The United Nations Association's Test of English

公益財団法人
日本国際連合協会 編著

国連英検
過去問題集
2019/2020 年度実施

A級

SANSHUSHA

はじめに
英語コミュニケーション能力の測定と国連英検

国連英検統括監修官　服部孝彦

　国連英検は，英語コミュニケーション能力を測るためのテストです。ひとくちにコミュニケーション能力をテストするといっても，「コミュニケーション能力」という概念は複雑です。ここでは，コミュニケーション能力の理論的枠組みをできる限り明らかにし，コミュニケーション能力をより的確に測るためのテストとしての国連英検のあり方について論じます。

　1960年代以降に言語研究に科学的な手法が求められるようになり，「コミュニケーション能力」という概念が生まれました。コミュニケーション能力の概念を最初に示したのはハイムズ（Hymes, 1972）ですが，それ以前に彼は，能力（competence）と運用（performance）の概念を提唱したチョムスキー（Chomsky, 1965）から大きな影響を受けたため，まずチョムスキーの言語理論から考察することにします。

　チョムスキーは，従来の学習を習慣形成による刺激と反応の結合が発達したもの，すなわち練習と強化によって形成された習慣とみなす行動主義（behaviorism）の考え方に異論を唱えました。彼は「具体的状況における実際の言語使用」（the actual use of language in concrete situation）を運用（performance）とし，それを「話者―聴者の言語の知識」（the speaker-hearer's knowledge of his language）である能力（competence）と区別しました。

　ハイムズはチョムスキーの能力（competence）の概念を発展させ，コミュニケーション能力（communicative competence）の概念を示しました。ハイムズは，文法的な意味に限定したチョムスキーの能力（competence）は不十分であるとし，能力を社会的文化的に拡張すると主張しました。ハイムズのコミュニケーション能力は次の4つに分類されます。

(1) Whether (and to what degree) something is formally possible;

(2) Whether (and to what degree) something is feasible in virtue of the means of implementation available;

(3) Whether (and to what degree) something is appropriate (adequate, happy, successful) in relation to a context in which it is used and evaluated;

(4) Whether (and to what degree) something is in fact done, actually performed, and what its doing entails.

　ハイムズは，文法的に正しいのか，発話することが現実的に可能か，社会的に適切であるか，実際に遂行されているのか，といった4つの基準を示したわけです。前者2つが文法に関するもので，後者2つが発話としての容認性に関するものであるといえます。

　ハイムズのコミュニケーション能力は，ウィドウソン（Widdowson, 1983），バックマン（Bachman, 1990），さらにはバックマンとパーマー（Bachman and Palmer, 1996）へと引き継がれました。「コミュニケーション能力」という用語は，communicative competence, communicative language ability, language ability と表記が変わり，定義も見直されました。コミュニケーション能力理論で最も新しいものは，バックマンの論理，およびバックマンとパーマーの理論です。バックマンとパーマー（Bachman and Palmer, 1996）の理論は，バックマン（Bachman, 1990）の理論を踏襲した改訂版で，テスティングのための理論という色彩を強めたものです。この2つの理論は現在，コミュニケーション理論の中で最も信頼のおけるものとして，言語教育で受け入れられています。

　バックマンとパーマーは，コミュニケーション能力に language ability という用語を用いています。そして，その language ability の中にハイムズやカネールとスウェインなどが言う communicative competence の構成要素をすべて含んだ言語知識（language knowledge）という概念を設けました。バックマンとパーマーの言語知識は，組織的知識（organizational knowledge）と語用論的知識（pragmatic knowledge）に分けられます。組織的知識はさらに，文法的知識（grammatical knowledge）とテキスト的知識（textual knowledge）に分類されます。語用論的知識は，機能的知識

(functional knowledge) と社会言語学的知識 (sociolinguistic knowledge) に分類されます。バックマンとパーマーは，言語知識以外にトピック知識（topical knowledge）や個人的特徴（personal characteristics）なども language ability の中に含まれる要素としており，これらすべてを結びつける能力として方略的能力（strategic competence）を挙げています。

　バックマンとパーマーは次のように述べ，自分たちが提示したコミュニケーションのモデルはテスト開発のためのものである，としています。

　　We would note that we conceive of this not as a working model of language processing, but rather as a conceptual basis for organizing our thinking about the test development process.

　バックマンとパーマーは，心理的な意味での言語処理モデルではなく，テスト開発のための概念的な枠組みを設定したといえます。

　バックマンとパーマーの language ability 理論の基礎になったのが，バックマン（Bachman, 1990）の communicative language ability 理論です。バックマンは，知識（knowledge）ではなく能力（competence）という用語を用いて，語用論的能力（pragmatic competence）と組織的能力（organizational competence）について，次のように述べています。

　　Pragmatic competence includes the types of knowledge which, in addition to organization competence, are employed in the contexturalized performance and interpretation of socially appropriate illocutionary acts in discourse.

　ここでバックマンは，語用論的能力／語用論的知識は，組織的能力／組織的知識の基盤の上にできあがるものであることを示しました。また，語用論的能力／語用論的知識は，テキストを構成しない一文単位でも発揮されるということを考えますと，組織的能力／組織的知識の中心は文法的能力／文法的知識であることがわかります。

　以上のコミュニケーション能力理論に基づき，国連英検では以下のように出題されています。中学校，高等学校で学習する英語の範囲内で出題さ

れるＣ級，Ｄ級，Ｅ級は，語用論的知識に先行して学習する必要のある組織的知識について問い，加えて組織的知識の基礎となる文法的知識を中心として出題しています。Ｂ級では，組織的知識の中の文法的知識に加え，英文エッセイをテーマに沿って"書く"問題も出題され，組織的知識の中のもう１つの力であるテキスト的知識も問われます。さらに，国連英検の特徴である国連に対する理解についての設問も出されます。特Ａ級とＡ級では，１次試験の筆記試験で文法的知識とテキスト的知識および国連に関する知識が問われ，１次試験合格者を対象に実施される２次試験の面接テストでは，これらに加えて語用論的知識である機能的知識と社会言語学的知識，言語力の要素を統合させる方略的能力，さらには国際事情についての知識も問われます。

　以上のように，国連英検ではコミュニケーション能力の研究成果を踏まえ，コミュニケーション能力の基盤をなす力を下の級で測定し，上の級ではそれらの基盤的な力の測定に加え，語用論的な力とメタ認知方略に関する力も測定しています。特に最上級の特Ａ級では，良識ある国際人として持つべき国際常識や国際適応能力についてもテストされます。国連英検は，まさしく総合的英語コミュニケーション能力を測定する試験であるといえます。

参考文献

Bachman, L. F. (1990). *Fundamental considerations in language testing*. Oxford: Oxford University Press.

Bachman, L. F & Palmer, A. S. (1996). *Language testing in practice*. Oxford: Oxford University Press.

Canale, M. (1983). On some dimensions of language proficiency. In J. Oller (Ed.) *Issues in language testing research*. (pp. 333-387). Massachusetts: Newburry House.

Canale, M. & Swain, M. (1980). Theoretical bases of communicative approaches to second language teaching and testing. *Applied Linguistics, 1* (1), 1-47.

Chomsky, N. (1965). *Aspects of the theory of syntax*. Cambridge, M.A.: The MIT Press.

Hymes, D. (1972). On communicative competence. In J. Pride & J. Holmes (Eds.) *Sociolinguistics: Selected readings*. (pp. 269-293). Harmondsworth: Penguin.

Widdowson, H. G. (1983). *Learning purpose and language use*. Oxford: Oxford University Press.

国連英検過去問題集　A級（2019-2020実施）

目次

はじめに	*3*
国連英検とは	*8*
A級のレベルと審査基準および問題の傾向と対策	*10*

2019年実施

第1回　問題	*12*
第1回　解答・解説	*36*
第2回　問題	*62*
第2回　解答・解説	*86*

2020年実施

第2回　問題	*112*
第2回　解答・解説	*136*

2次試験（面接テスト）について	*160*
国連英検実施要項	*163*
著者・執筆協力者プロフィール	*166*

※本書は，実際の検定試験で使用された試験問題に基づいて編
　集されておりますが，一部修正されている場合があります。

国連英検とは

■「国連英検」（国際連合公用語英語検定試験）は，1981年に始まり，長い歴史を持つ英語検定試験です。試験は年に2回，全国主要都市で実施されます。特A級からE級まで全部で6つの級があり，中学生から社会人，シニアエイジまでの幅広い層を対象とし，受験資格は特になく，どなたでも受験できます。

　試験を主催するのは，外務省の外郭団体としてスタートした公益財団法人日本国際連合協会です。日本国際連合協会は，国連のA級諮問民間団体である「国連協会世界連盟」（WFUNA）の有力メンバーで，国内外での国連普及活動を積極的に行っています。

　国連英検も国連普及活動の一環として実施されており，国連の理念である「国際協力」「国際理解」をコンセプトに，「真に役立つグローバルコミュニケーション能力」の育成を目標としています。試験内容は国連の活動に沿って，世界平和，地球環境，世界政治，世界経済から，人権，食品，医療などの世界情勢，国際時事問題まで幅広く出題されるため，今まさに地球上で問われている問題を認識し，自分の考えや解決策を論理的に伝達する表現力が求められます。単なる語学力の判定にとどまらず，総合的な国際コミュニケーションスキルが問われます。

■ 国連英検は，資格として多角度にアピールできる検定試験です。多くの大学で推薦入試・編入試験の評価資格として認められ，B級以上の合格を単位認定している大学もあります。

　特A級は，成績優秀者に外務大臣賞が授与されるほか，合格者には外務省国際機関人事センターが実施している「JPO派遣候補者選考試験」において加点が行われます。

　このJPOは，国際公務員（国連職員・ユネスコ職員など）になるための登竜門と言えるもので，2年間の海外派遣を経て国際公務員試験に挑戦できる制度です。

Ａ級は成績優秀者に国連協会会長賞が授与されます。

　Ｃ級以上の合格者は，文部科学省より，高等学校卒業程度認定規則において，英語資格としてレベル認定されています。

　また，国際協力機構（JICA）では，Ｃ級以上の合格者を，応募の際に必要となる語学力の評価基準をクリアしたものと認定しています。

　なお，警視庁では警察官採用試験（1次試験）に「資格経歴等の評定」を導入していますが，国連英検Ｃ級以上の合格者については，1次試験の成績の一部として評価しています。

■ 国連英検は，コミュニケーションを重視した試験です。Ｂ級〜Ｅ級で出題されるリスニング問題のウェイトは40％と高く，またＢ級以上は国際時事問題をテーマとした英作文（ウェイト20％）が設けられています。Ａ級以上は2次試験で面接試験を実施し，ネイティブスピーカーと国際時事問題について討論を行います。さらに特Ａ級については，ネイティブスピーカーに加え，元外務省大使など外交実務経験者や国際関係を研究する大学教授を面接官として，より深い議論を行います。

● 2020年第1回の国連英検中止について
　同回の検定試験は，新型コロナウイルス感染症拡大防止の観点から，中止されました。そのため，本書には2020年第1回の問題・解説は掲載されていません。

● 国連英検受験（Ｃ級以上）のための指定テキストについて
　現在は『新 わかりやすい国連の活動と世界』（三修社）が指定テキストになっていますが，2019年第1回までは『わかりやすい国連の活動と世界［改訂版］』（三修社）が指定テキストであったため，本書の問題・解説もそれに基づいて作成されています。

● Ａ級のレベルと審査基準および問題の傾向と対策 ●

レベルと審査基準

　問題の形式と内容が異なるため，他の英語検定試験との比較は困難ですが，国連英検Ａ級は実用英語検定１級とほぼ同じ，あるいはそれより高いレベルといってよいでしょう。英字新聞や雑誌の記事を限られた時間内で理解できる，比較的高度な語句や表現を認識できる，またはあるテーマについて論理的な内容を英文で表現する，日常の身辺の出来事・時事問題などに関して，国籍や文化背景を異にする人々を交えて討議する能力も要求されます。

問題の傾向と対策

　１次試験は，マークシートによる客観テスト（80点）と英作文（20点）から成り立っています（リスニングテストはありません）。

　客観テストでは特Ａ級と同じく，8題の大問が出されます。最初の大問は国連に関するものですので，指定テキストの『新 わかりやすい国連の活動と世界』*New Today's Guide to the United Nations*（三修社）を読んでおくことが課題になっています。各級の指定テキストからの出題範囲は国連英検のホームページに掲載されています。各題の英文の長さは約400〜1000語程度で，速読が求められます。その他の大問のトピックも特Ａ級と同じく，国際問題・政治・経済・歴史・文化・科学や小説などが出題されます。

　英作文では，約150〜200語程度の英文を作成できる知識・思考力・表現力が要求され，受験者の意見の有無も考慮されます。

　２次試験は１次試験合格者が対象の面接試験で，約10分間，ネイティブスピーカーとディスカッションを行います。

　面接でカバーされるトピックは主に，国連の理念と活動・時事問題・自己紹介・日常の事柄についてで，発音や文法のチェック・知識・判断力・表現力・マナーなどが審査されます。実施の詳細はp.160をご参照ください。

2019年

第1回試験

問題

A級

外務省後援
２０１９年度第１回国際連合公用語
英語検定試験 (120分)

受験上の注意

1. 問題用紙は試験開始の合図があるまで開いてはいけません。その間に、この**受験上の注意を熟読**しておいてください。

2. **受験番号と氏名を解答用紙（マークシートと作文用紙）に記入してください。**

3. 答案用紙の配布は１人１部のみです。複数の配布は致しません。

4. 試験開始前は、答案への解答記入は禁止です。

5. マークシートの記入は、１～100までの記入箇所がありますが、この級では１～80までを使います。

6. マークシートの記入は、必ずＨＢ以上の濃い鉛筆を使って該当箇所を黒く塗りつぶしてください。書き間違いの場合は「アト」が残らないように消してください。マークシートは絶対に折ったり曲げたりしないでください。

7. 受験級、受験地区、会場番号、受験番号のマークシートへの記入は監督者の指示に従い、間違いなく記入してください。**(裏表紙の「マークシート記入例」参照)**

8. 作文は、⑴読みやすい文字をペン、ボールペンまたはＨＢ以上の濃い鉛筆で書いてください。⑵使用語数の150～200語を目安にしてください。

9. 試験問題についての質問は、印刷が不鮮明な場合を除き、一切受けつけません。

10. 中途退室の際は、マークシートと作文用紙を持って監督者に渡し、他の受験者の迷惑にならないように静かに退室してください。中途退室後の再入室はできません。

11. 試験中は他の受験者の妨げとなる行動は慎んでください。また携帯電話等の電源はお切りください。

12. マークシートと作文用紙は監督者に提出し、問題用紙はご自由にお持ち帰りください。

＊試験問題の複製や転載、インターネットへのアップロード等、いかなる媒体への転用を禁止します。

試験結果について

1. 第１次試験の結果は2019年６月26日㈬頃に受験申込書に記載された住所に郵送で通知します。

2. その間に住所変更をされた方は、郵便局へ住所変更の届け出を忘れずに行ってください。

3. 発表前の試験結果のお問合せには応じられません。

第２次試験について

1. 第１次試験合格者には、試験結果発表と同時に試験日時、会場を指定して通知します。（第１次試験を特別会場で受験した合格者には最寄りの２次試験会場が指定されます。）

2. 第２次試験は2019年７月14日㈰です。A級の試験地は札幌・仙台・東京・名古屋・大阪・福岡・鹿児島・沖縄のいずれかになります。（特A級との併願で特A級の第１次試験に合格された方の試験地は東京と大阪になります。）あらかじめご了承願います。

公益財団法人 日本国際連合協会
http://www.unaj.or.jp/

I. Fill in each of the following blanks with the most appropriate of the four alternatives according to the knowledge and information gained from Today's Guide to the United Nations.

1. At its session in _____, the Assembly decided to celebrate the fortieth anniversary of the United Nations by a series of special commemorative meetings, culminating in the proclamation, on 24 October, of an International Year of Peace.
   A. 1985   B. 1986   C. 1987   D. 1988

2. _____ is not specifically described in the UN Charter, but it has evolved over the past 40 years as an internationally accepted way of controlling conflicts and promoting the peaceful settlement or disputes.
   A. Peacebuilding   B. Intervention
   C. Mediation   D. Peacekeeping

3. When a UN Member State or group of States, or the Secretary-General, proposes establishment of a peacekeeping operation, _____ basic conditions have to be met.
   A. two   B. three   C. four   D. five

4. Article 30 warns that no State, group or person may claim any right, under the Declaration, "to engage in any activity or to perform any act aimed at the _____ of any of the rights and freedoms set forth" in the Declaration.
   A. intrusion   B. deprivation
   C. destruction   D. violation

5. The General Assembly meets once a year in regular session, commencing on _____ in September and continuing until mid-December.
   A. the second Tuesday   B. the third Tuesday
   C. the second Thursday   D. the third Thursday

6. The World Food Conference was convened by the General Assembly in _____ in 1974 to develop ways for the international community as a whole to take action to resolve the world food problem within the broader context of development and international economic cooperation.
   A. Bucharest   B. Stockholm
   C. Rome   D. Nairobi

7.   The basic function of _____ is to extend international protection to refugees who, by definition, do not enjoy the protection of their former home country.
    A.   UNCTAD   B.   UNFPA
    C.   UNHCR   D.   UNICEF

8.   The 51 original Members of the United Nations were the States that took part in the _____ Conference or had previously signed the Declaration by United Nations, and which signed and ratified the charter.
    A.   San Francisco   B.   Cairo
    C.   Yalta   D.   Potsdam

9.   In _____ the General Assembly adopted a Declaration on Measures to Eliminate International Terrorism, which condemned all acts and practices of terrorism as criminal and unjustifiable, wherever and by whomever they were committed.
    A.   1992   B.   1993   C.   1994   D.   1995

10. Since its early days, the United Nations, carrying out the pledge in _____ of the Charter to "promote higher standards of living, full employment and conditions of economic and social progress and development", has supported the development efforts of the poorer countries.
    A.   Article 22   B.   Article 33
    C.   Article 44   D.   Article 55

II. Choose from among the four alternatives the one that is the most appropriate form of each of the underlined verbs.

An international group of public health experts on Monday called on the World Health Organization **(11) convene** an emergency committee to consider declaring Congo's Ebola outbreak an international public health emergency.

The group of experts wrote in the Lancet that such a call would help **(12) galvanize** "high-level political, financial, and technical support to address the Ebola outbreak that started last May."

The outbreak, declared just over six months ago in Congo's east, is the country's tenth and the world's second largest **(13) record**. Instability, dense populations, political instability and mass displacement have contributed to the spread of the disease.

"The epidemic is not under control, and has a high risk of spread to the region, perhaps globally," said lead author Lawrence Gostin, faculty director of Georgetown University's O'Neill Institute for National and Global Health Law.

The experts pointed specifically to concerns of Ebola **(14) spread** to nearby countries such as South Sudan, which they say is among the most fragile states in the world with far less capacity to control an Ebola outbreak.

"**(15) Take** bold measures to prevent the spread of the disease in this country where violence is prevalent, and a famine is predicted, is critical to preventing a humanitarian disaster," Gostin said.

The experts argue that the criteria for declaring an international emergency have been met, including public health impact, novelty and scale and movement of people.

The World Health Organization on Monday responded that the WHO and its partners in Congo and neighboring countries **(16) continue** to closely monitor the situation for signs that an expert committee meeting would be needed.

"If and when we see those signs, the director general will call a meeting," said WHO spokesman Tarik Jasarevic.

The first meeting of the Emergency Committee, **(17) charge** with making the call of a public emergency, took place Oct. 17.

The call to attention comes as, six months on, Ebola has spread to 18 health zones in Congo, and though many initial hotspots have been contained, new ones have popped up in recent weeks.

Despite their call Monday, however, the group of experts also **(18) warn** that a declaration of an international public health emergency may also have negative consequences, such as a ban on trade or travel barriers in Congo. So it also called on the WHO and United Nations to "take active steps to prevent unlawful and harmful restrictions including calling out countries that violate laws **(19) design** to prevent this sort of unwarranted action," according to Gostin.

In October, the emergency committee determined that it was particularly important that no international travel or trade restrictions (**20**) **apply**, and neighboring countries accelerate their preparedness and surveillance.

| 11. | A. | which convene | B. | convening |
| | C. | to convene | D. | convened |

| 12. | A. | galvanized | B. | galvanize |
| | C. | and galvanize | D. | galvanizing |

| 13. | A. | recorded | B. | to record |
| | C. | recording | D. | record |

| 14. | A. | which spread | B. | spreads |
| | C. | spreading | D. | spread |

| 15. | A. | Taking | B. | When taking |
| | C. | Having taken | D. | Take |

| 16. | A. | continuing | B. | to continue |
| | C. | had continued | D. | continue |

| 17. | A. | is charged | B. | charging |
| | C. | which are charged | D. | charged |

| 18. | A. | warning | B. | warned |
| | C. | to warn | D. | was warned |

| 19. | A. | designed | B. | have designed |
| | C. | designing | D. | to design |

| 20. | A. | have been applied | B. | to be applied |
| | C. | be applied | D. | applied |

Ⅲ. Fill in each of the following blanks with the most grammatically and logically appropriate of the four alternatives.

"In my opening statement to this conference one week ago... I warned **(21)** _____ _____ and that Katowice must — in no uncertain terms — be a success, as a necessary platform to reverse this trend," said Secretary-General Guterres.

Since 2 December, the conference has brought together thousands of climate action decision-makers, advocates and activists, with one key objective: adopting global guidelines for the 197 parties of the 2015 Paris Agreement, when countries committed to limiting global warming to less than 2°C – and as close as possible to 1.5° – above pre-industrial levels.

With only **(22)** _____, the UN chief regretted that "despite progress in the negotiating texts, much remains to be done". On Wednesday, given the complex state of discussions, the Polish Presidency of COP24 proposed a text to act as a "new basis for negotiations".

"Key political issues remain unresolved," said Mr. Guterres. "This is not surprising—we recognize the complexity of this work. But we are running out of time," he warned, **(23)** _____ issued in October by the Intergovernmental Panel on Climate Change (IPCC).

"Over the last 10 days", he said, addressing the country delegations, which are locked in negotiations, "many of you have worked long, hard hours and I want to acknowledge your efforts. But we need to **(24)** _____ ____ to follow-up on the commitments made in Paris."

He called on negotiators to boost their ambition, with regards to "predictable and accessible financial flows for the economic transition towards a low-emission and climate-resilient world."

The Secretary-General reminded the **(25)** _____ _____ support the efforts of developing countries, as established by the UN Climate Change Convention (UNFCCC), under which the Paris Agreement falls, and which was signed in 1992, more than 25 years ago.

"It's very **(26)** _____ of climate change that we have not managed to find predictable support for the actions that must be taken," he remarked.

Mr. Guterres **(27)** _____ COP24, including by the World Bank, multilateral development banks, and the private sector. However, he urged developed nations to "scale up their contributions to jointly mobilize $100 billion annually by 2020", as laid out three years ago in Paris.

In addition to increased resources, the UN Secretary-General also called for the development of a "flexible but robust set of rules" to implement the Paris Agreement – as

2018 was set by the UNFCCC parties themselves, as the deadline for these guidelines, so countries can move forward with climate action in a transparent way.

"Countries have different realities, different capacities and different circumstances," noted the UN chief, as he explained that "we **(28)** _____ _____ all countries" and that is "fair and effective for all".

To achieve this, Mr. Guterres stressed the importance of building trust through a "strong transparency framework to monitor and assess progress on all fronts: mitigation, adaptation and provision of support, including finance, technology and capacity building".

The UN chief said we have the know-how, as well as "incredible momentum from all segments of society" adding that "what we need, is the political will to move forward".

"I understand that none of this is easy. I understand some **(29)** _____ _____ decisions," he acknowledged, "But this is the time for consensus. This is the time for political compromises to be reached. This means sacrifices, but it will benefit us all collectively."

Challenging the delegates and ministers to overcome their national preferences and work "together" and "finish the job" with raised ambition "on all fronts", Mr. Guterres concluded: "To waste this opportunity in Katowice **(30)** _____ _____ climate change. It would not only be immoral, it would be suicidal."

21. A. climate that running is change faster than we are
B. running is faster than climate change that we are
C. that climate change is running faster than we are
D. we are that faster than climate change is running

22. A. days for the negotiations three left at the conference
B. for the negotiations three days the conference left at
C. the conference negotiations at the left for three days
D. three days left at the conference for the negotiations

23. A. alarming special warming report on referring to the global
B. on referring to global the warming alarming special report
C. referring to the alarming special report on global warming
D. to report on referring the special global alarming warming

24. A. accelerate those efforts to reach consensus if we want
B. consensus those efforts if we want accelerate to reach
C. reach accelerate those efforts we want to consensus if
D. want those efforts reach to consensus if we accelerate

25. A. audience that developed countries had a financial obligation to
     B. countries audience that had a financial obligation to developed
     C. developed countries audience financial that had a obligation to
     D. that audience financial countries had a developed obligation to

26. A. those suffering to explain the effects to from difficult
     B. suffering from the difficult effects to those to explain
     C. effects from difficult suffering to explain to those the
     D. difficult to explain to those suffering from the effects

27. A. financial announcements made the hailed various of beginning since
     B. hailed various financial announcements made since the beginning of
     C. made various of announcements beginning since the hailed financial
     D. since the announcements hailed various of financial beginning made

28. A. balances a formula of the responsibilities must find that
     B. find the responsibilities of a formula that balances must
     C. must find a formula that balances the responsibilities of
     D. of the formula must find a balances that responsibilities

29. A. need to make you tough of some political will
     B. of you will need to make some tough political
     C. tough need will make to you some political of
     D. will make tough political need of you to some

30. A. compromises our last best chance to stop runaway
     B. stop runaway compromises best to last chance our
     C. runaway our compromises stop to last best chance
     D. chance to stop our last runaway compromises best

19

IV. Choose from among the four alternatives the one that best completes the following sentence.

31. The prime ministers of Japan and the Netherlands said Wednesday they want Britain's withdrawal _____ the European Union to go as smoothly as possible and to prevent Brexit from happening _____ an agreement on future ties between the bloc and its former member.
   A. for – in   B. by – under
   C. from – without   D. into – on

32. As the United States has increasingly _____ from multilateral leadership and engagement at the United Nations, China in particular has stepped up to _____ the vacuum, according to diplomats and insiders, while countries such as Japan are left on uncertain footing.
   A. retrieved – leave   B. stemmed – legitimate
   C. reeled – uplift   D. backed away – fill

33. Venezuelan military officers blocked a bridge on the border with Colombia _____ an anticipated humanitarian aid shipment Tuesday as opposition leader Juan Guaido stepped up his _____ to President Nicolas Maduro's authority.
   A. ahead of – challenge   B. in terms of – contingency
   C. in contrast to – efforts D. in danger of – crackdowns

34. The United Nations Secretary-General António Guterres congratulated the Greek Parliament over its _____ of a name change for the former Yugoslav Republic of Macedonia on Friday, and commended the leaders of both countries for _____ the end to a naming dispute that has roiled the region for some 28 years.
   A. ratification – signaling B. affirmation – galvanizing
   C. provocation – diffusing   D. cessation – manifesting

35. The West needs to understand that the challenge of China's technological revolution runs much deeper than Huawei's _____ with the United States over intellectual property theft and _____ espionage, one of Britain's top spies said.
   A. reconciliation – insurgent B. agreement – industrial
   C. row – state   D. deportation – dormant

36. With the eighth anniversary of Syria's brutal civil conflict _____, the new United Nations Special Envoy to Syria gave his first briefing to the Security Council on the complex political road map towards ending the war, with a pledge to work "_____ and diligently".
   A. menacing − unconditionally   B. looming − impartially
   C. dominating − immensely   D. commemorating − regularly

37. Thousands of Sudanese rallied on Thursday in some of the most widespread protests of a two-month _____ against President Omar al-Bashir, as emergency courts tried hundreds late into the night and Bashir _____ his powers as head of the ruling party to its deputy.
   A. uprising − relinquished   B. disorder − seized
   C. setback − entrusted   D. revolt − delegated

38. The top United Nations human rights official has strongly _____ the suicide bomb attack against Indian security forces in Pulwama district of Jammu and Kashmir on 14 February and has called on authorities to bring those responsible to _____.
   A. convicted − ruin   B. decried − effect
   C. accused − standstill   D. condemned − justice

39. Caterpillar Inc. trucks, Xerox Corp. machines and Samsonite International SA luggage are among U.S. goods that would face _____ European Union tariffs should U.S. President Donald Trump follow through on a threat to _____ automotive duties against the bloc, according to a senior EU official.
   A. punitive − decree   B. unanimous − reckon
   C. retaliatory − impose   D. preferential − promulgate

40. While the Nicaraguan Government claims to want to resolve its political and social _____, dissenters continue to be arrested and convicted, clearly hindering a _____ environment for "genuine and inclusive dialogue," the United Nations rights chief said on Friday.
   A. unrest − conducive   B. adversary − favorable
   C. backlash − secure   D. collusion − fragile

21

V. **Choose from among the underlined phrases the one that is grammatically or idiomatically incorrect.**

41. The number of (**A**) <u>casualties in Afghanistan from</u> landmines and (**B**) <u>other explosives has larger than</u> tripled since 2012, the UN said on Wednesday, (**C**) <u>in support of a call to</u> provide (**D**) <u>more long-term support for</u> survivors.

42. The UN Secretary-General (**A**) <u>said on Saturday he was</u> "deeply shocked" (**B**) <u>by a deadly mass-shooting inside a</u> synagogue in the US city (**C**) <u>of</u> <u>Pittsburgh, which reportedly left</u> 11 people (**D**) <u>dead and several others wound,</u> some critically.

43. Japan (**A**) <u>has decided to withdraw the</u> International Whaling Commission (**B**) <u>in a bid to resume commercial</u> whaling (**C**) <u>for the first time in</u> 30 years, (**D**) <u>government sources said</u> Thursday.

44. The number of people moving into the Tokyo metropolitan region (**A**) <u>in 2018</u> exceeded the number (**B**) <u>moving out by nearly 140,000, a government report</u> showed Thursday, despite (**C**) <u>of Prime Minister Shinzo Abe's plan</u> (**D**) <u>to</u> <u>reverse the trend by 2020 to</u> revive rural areas.

45. Okinawa Gov. Denny Tamaki (**A**) <u>has clarified his intention to</u> hold a referendum (**B**) <u>over the relocation of</u> a key U.S. military base within the prefecture on Feb. 24 (**C**) <u>as planned — even without the</u> participation of five (**D**) <u>municipalities which assemblies have</u> not approved related budgets.

46. Japan is considering (**A**) <u>to hold informal talks with</u> South Korea and other countries (**B**) <u>on a dispute over the name of</u> the Sea of Japan, a top official has hinted, (**C**) <u>in what could become the latest</u> (**D**) <u>in a series of diplomatic</u> <u>feuds between</u> Tokyo and Seoul.

47. Government-led (**A**) <u>relief efforts are stepping up</u> (**B**) <u>at the tip of the</u> <u>Indonesia's two main islands</u> of Sumatra (**C**) <u>and Java after a tsunami slammed</u> <u>into</u> (**D**) <u>densely-populated coastal areas along the</u> Sunda Strait on Saturday night.

48. The United Nations refugee agency (UNHCR), (**A**) <u>on the last day of 2018, called</u> <u>on</u> (**B**) <u>UN Member States to urgent offer</u> safe ports (**C**) <u>of disembarkation</u> <u>for 49 refugees and</u> migrants, (**D**) <u>including young children, aboard</u> rescue vessels in the Mediterranean Sea.

49. The findings of a new UN-backed report, released on Monday, **(A)** <u>showing the</u> <u>ongoing healing of</u> the ozone layer, **(B)** <u>are being hailed as a demonstration of</u> <u>what</u> global agreements can achieve, **(C)** <u>and an inspiration for more ambitious</u> <u>climate</u> action **(D)** <u>to halt a catastrophic raise in</u> world temperatures.

50. **(A)** <u>Options under consideration for the</u> next Imperial era name, which will **(B)** <u>be unveiled April 1, is believed to</u> include terms adapted **(C)** <u>from</u> <u>Japanese classics despite past era names</u> **(D)** <u>typically being drawn from</u> <u>Chinese classics,</u> government sources have said.

VI. Choose from among the four alternatives the one that most closely corresponds to the meaning of words in bold type and blanks in the following passage.

In today's world, there are numerous examples of popular demand for political change. They generally arise at a time when politicians seem unable to deliver on their promises. Take, for example, the year 2008—described by Amartya Sen (2009) as 'a year of crises'. There was a spike in oil prices that raised the cost of fuel and petroleum products globally and, in the autumn of 2008, there was an economic crisis in the United States that quickly spread, compounding prior issues, and the global economy **(51) faltered**.

The United States is a country that allows its citizens full participation in politics—a place where the people determine the direction of the nation via their mass participation in elections. Such slogans as 'land of the free' and 'anyone can be president' come to mind. But, like many other similar political regimes, it faces **(52)** _____ into a system that favours the rich. In the US today, the top one per cent of people are in receipt of 21 per cent of national income. Over time, this proportion has been changing for the worse. In the 1970s the top one per cent's income share was 'only' about 10 per cent. The issue became acute following the 2008 financial crisis, which laid bare the degree of inequality in American society and the lack of influence over public policy felt by the majority of the population (see Picketty 2014). Two million Americans lost their homes in the so-called 'sub-prime mortgage' collapse, which then spiralled into a much bigger crisis affecting the entire financial system. The US government **(53) bailed out** some large corporations and banks to the tune of hundreds of billions of dollars to prevent the whole financial system from collapsing. This was accompanied by austerity measures that eroded benefits and public services as the government had less money available due to the economic crash. This general pattern was also seen in other liberal economies, including the United Kingdom. **(54)** _____, a picture emerged in some circles that the government had given money to the richest and taken money from the poorest. The Occupy movement was a diffuse and diverse reaction to this perception. It was a reaction against the ineffectiveness of the traditional tools of democratic politics and government such as political parties, elections and lobbying.

The Occupy movement protested against Wall Street, home of the US financial industry, as a symbol of 'unearned' privilege and wealth—even though it was politicians who were **(55) coming up with** and implementing austerity cuts. The movement began in Zuccotti Park, near Wall Street, on 17 September 2011. Critics noted the activists' lack of a clear set of demands and their tendency to only highlight grievances. However, a clear set of values did emerge: Solidarity—society's institutions should aim to maximise mutual benefits; Diversity—diverse solutions to pressing problems; Equity—in terms of solutions and distribution; and Control—especially self-management, freedom and autonomy.

Following the emergence of the Occupy movement, there were hundreds of similar occupations all over the world—though mainly in the United States and Western Europe.

Years later, it remains clear that the problems that prompted these protests have not gone away. However, much of the energy has **(56) dissipated** from the movement. This is partly because the protesters could not develop and articulate a common platform that would enable a clear pathway to action to be advanced (which would have been the priority of a political party or revolutionary movement). Instead, they just produced a slogan, 'We are the 99%', highlighting the growth of inequality since the 1970s that disproportionately affects women, young people and minorities. The Occupy movement **(57) splintered** following the decision of the mayor of New York to break up the protest in November 2011. Without leaders or specific demands, it turned into an unfocused protest against everything that was 'wrong' with the world.

While the Occupy movement's social critique resonates with many people, the question remains whether it offers a practical and achievable means to accomplish goals. How best to **(58) mobilise** people to alleviate poverty? Many would argue that action aimed at poverty alleviation—for example, building public housing projects or preventing cuts to food stamps—has to involve mainstream politics. Critics claim that the new generation of activists may have forgotten, abandoned or overlooked the progressive ideal of a reform-minded government raising up the poor and mitigating discrimination. What is clear is that the Occupy movement has given voice to concerns about systemic divisions in the economic and social structure in the United States and other Western states. These concerns **(59) touch a nerve** that continues to resonate—much like the aftermath of the Umbrella Revolution in Hong Kong. And, also like Hong Kong, the adverse reaction of certain political leaders and senior police officers suggested to some the hypocrisy of those with power. Post-2008, it is now common for politicians seeking election in the United States to profess their support for 'main street' rather than Wall Street as a means of **(60)** _____ popular support.

51. **In this context, "faltered" could best be replaced with**
   A. dithered
   C. lingered
   B. paused
   D. shuddered

52. **From the context, the underlined blank could best be filled with**
   A. burgeoning
   C. relapsing
   B. degenerating
   D. withering

53. **In this context, "bailed out" could best be replaced with**
   A. held back
   C. pulled out of
   B. cut off
   D. shored up

25

54. **From the context, the underlined blank could best be filled with**

A. Hence   B. Henceforth

C. Like this   D. Successively

55. **In this context, "coming up with" could best be replaced with**

A. constructing   B. devising

C. fabricating   D. promising

56. **In this context, "dissipated" is closest in meaning to**

A. depleted   B. exhaled

C. separated   D. vaporized

57. **In this context, "splintered" is closest in meaning to**

A. expelled   B. discharged

C. fragmented   D. stumbled

58. **In this context, "mobilise" is closest in meaning to**

A. assemble   B. convene

C. incite   D. stimulate

59. **In this context, "touch a nerve" is closest in meaning to**

A. reflect a sensitive topic   B. represent an unachievable outcome

C. require a harsh reaction   D. reveal a crucial turning point

60. **From the context, the underlined blank could best be filled with**

A. contradicting   B. disputing

C. pronouncing   D. rallying

Ⅶ. Choose from among the four alternatives the one that best explains each of the underlined words or phrases in the context of the article below.

More than one billion 12 to 35-year-olds risk irreversible hearing loss from exposure to loud sounds such as music played on their smartphone, UN health experts said on Tuesday, (**61**) **unveiling** new guidelines to help address the problem.

The recommendations to prevent noise-induced hearing loss and related conditions such as tinnitus – commonly experienced as a ringing sound inside the ear - include better functions on personal audio devices that monitor how loud, and for how long, people listen to music.

The WHO-@ITU #SafeListening standard recommends that personal audio devices include "sound allowance" function: software that (**62**) **tracks** the level and (**63**) **duration** of the user's exposure to sound.

"Over a billion young people are at risk of hearing loss simply by doing what they really enjoy doing a lot, which is listening regularly to music through their headphones over their devices," said Dr Shelly Chadha, a Technical Officer, working on preventing deafness and hearing loss, at the WHO.

"At the moment, we (**64**) **don't really have anything solid** other than our instinct to tell us: are we doing this right, or is this something that is going to lead to tinnitus and hearing loss a few years (**65**) **down the line**?"

The joint World Health Organization (WHO) and International Telecommunications Union (ITU) initiative is an attempt to (**66**) **tackle** the lack of awareness about what constitutes too much noise, amid data showing that around 50 per cent of young people listen to unsafe levels of sound through personal audio devices including smartphones, whose use continues to grow globally.

Today, hearing loss which is not addressed is estimated to cost the global economy $750 million, the WHO says.

(**67**) "**Think of it like** driving on a highway but without a speedometer in your car or a speed limit," Dr Chadha explained. "And what we have proposed is that your smartphone comes fitted with a speedometer, with a measurement system that tells you how much sound you're getting and tells you if you're going over the limit."

A parental volume control option is also included in the UN recommendations to industry, which participated in two years of discussions, along with experts from government, consumer bodies and civil society.

The guidelines also propose using technology to generate individualized listener profiles by monitoring how much people use their audio devices, then letting them know how safely – or not – they have been listening.

"What we propose are certain features like automatic limiting of, or automatic volume reduction and parental control of the volume," explained Dr Chadha, "So that when somebody goes over their sound limit they have the option that the device will

27

automatically reduce the volume to a level which is not going to harm their ears."

According to the WHO, more than one in 20 people – 432 million adults and 34 million children – has disabling hearing loss, which impacts on their quality of life.

Most sufferers live in poor and middle-income countries, the UN agency notes, adding that by 2050, more than 900 million people will have **(68) significantly** impaired hearing.

Around half of all cases of hearing loss could be prevented through public health **(69) measures**, the WHO insists, its recommendations coming ahead of World Hearing Day on Sunday 3 March.

(70) "Given that we have the technological know-how to prevent hearing loss, it should not be the case that so many young people continue to damage their hearing while listening to music," said Tedros Adhanom Ghebreyesus, WHO Director-General. "They must understand that once they lose their hearing, it won't come back."

61. **unveiling**

A.	concealing	B.	introducing
C.	obscuring	D.	suppressing

62. **tracks**

A.	foils	B.	forbids
C.	follows	D.	forces

63. **duration**

A.	discomfort	B.	enjoyment
C.	humor	D.	length

64. **don't really have anything solid**

A.	can't show clear proof	B.	couldn't be more sure
C.	don't like any music	D.	wouldn't listen to you

65. **down the line**

A.	backward in time	B.	before any damage
C.	forming a queue	D.	in the future

66. **tackle**

A.	challenge	B.	maintain
C.	preserve	D.	support

67. **Think of it like**

A.	Avoid never being	B.	Imagine you are
C.	Pretend you adore	D.	Don't mind going

28

68. <u>significantly</u>

    A. immaterially   B. triflingly

    C. trivially   D. palpably

69. <u>measures</u>

    A. fatigue   B. practices

    C. stupor   D. torpor

70. <u>Given that</u>

    A. Inside   B. Never

    C. Since   D. Someday

Fill in each of the following blanks with the most appropriate of the four alternatives as required by the context.

Juan Guaido's first stop after he skipped out of Venezuela last week was Colombia. But after he failed to push food and medicine across the borders to hasten the end of **(71)** _____ President Nicolas Maduro's rule, he headed to Brazil.

He was in Argentina Friday following meetings in Paraguay, and is heading to Ecuador today to be received by President Lenin Moreno. Peru's President Martin Viscarra has also invited Guaido to Lima, according to the deputy foreign minister.

The opposition leader insists he'll be home soon, but his lengthening regional tour raises questions about just how and when he intends to get back to Caracas. Guaido, head of the opposition-dominated National Assembly, risks not only being blocked from re-entering Venezuela, but being tossed into jail after violating a foreign-travel ban. Meanwhile, the amnesty he promised military officers who join him **(72)** _____ in his own legislature and resurgent street protests have lost their focal point.

The U.S., which along with some 50 other nations recognizes Guaido as Venezuela's rightful leader after sham elections, has threatened severe repercussions if Maduro takes direct action against his chief rival. **(73)** _____, Venezuela's ruling socialists have already exiled and thrown hundreds of dissidents behind bars.

Guaido, a 35-year-old congressman, says his tour is meant to deepen ties with allies and plan how to defeat a dictatorship. Yet the longer he stays abroad, the more the likelihood that his movement to unseat Maduro will lose momentum **(74)** _____ the effort to bring humanitarian aid into Venezuela was brutally crushed last week.

"We will be back in Caracas very soon to continue the work we swore to do for all of Venezuela," he said in Asuncion following a closed door meeting with President Mario Abdo Benitez.

Later Friday, Guaido flew to Argentina where he was received by President Mauricio Macri. Following a roughly 30-minute meeting with Argentina's leader, Guaido again said he'd return home in the coming days and that the National Assembly on Saturday would announce dates for protests against the government. He also **(75)** _____ another concern.

"Intervention in Venezuela is not like delivering a pizza, it takes much responsibility," Guaido said. "Nobody wants the use of force."

Guaido is analyzing the effect of a potential jailing, while the government considers the repercussions of throwing him behind bars, said Felix Seijas, head of the Caracas polling firm Delphos.

"For the government, the best case scenario is that Guaido doesn't return," Seijas said. In visiting allies, "Guaido is trying to raise the **(76)** _____ of being imprisoned."

Guaido told the news agency Infobae on Saturday that his arrest in Venezuela would lead to a "popular uprising."

Yet, the opposition had billed last Saturday as a day that would break Maduro's grip by ushering aid into a hungry nation. But still-loyal police and soldiers repelled thousands of activists moving food and medicine stockpiled at international crossings, heeding the Maduro government warning that the effort was the **(77)** _____ to an invasion.

They set loose volleys of tear gas, plastic pellets and bullets, killing at least four, injuring hundreds and leaving Guaido stuck outside his country. On Friday, the Trump administration sanctioned six security officers "**(78)** _____ the reprehensible violence, tragic deaths, and unconscionable torching of food and medicine destined for sick and starving Venezuelans," Treasury Secretary Steven Mnuchin said in a statement.

More than 500 members of the security forces have deserted to Colombia since Saturday, but not a single high-ranking officer who commands troops has switched sides. Further complicating matters, a bill to give members of the military amnesty for corruption and rights abuses if they defect has **(79)** _____ in Guaido's own National Assembly amid a backlash from hard-line lawmakers who say it's too forgiving.

As Guaido travels, the regime has extended carnival holidays, urging Venezuelans to leave the cities for the beach. Guaido, meanwhile, says he will rally supporters when he arrives and is promising to announce another wave of protests.

"We will continue to occupy the streets of Venezuela **(80)** _____ the threats to our lives," he said in Asuncion.

71.	A.	shrewd	B.	autocratic	
	C.	egalitarian	D.	rampant	
72.	A.	languishes	B.	grants	
	C.	accelerates	D.	stirs	
73.	A.	Furthermore	B.	In retrospect	
	C.	Still	D.	Instead	
74.	A.	if	B.	after	
	C.	while	D.	until	
75.	A.	addressed	B.	rendered	
	C.	expedited	D.	caused	
76.	A.	status quo	B.	deficit	
	C.	stakes	D.	reservation	
77.	A.	wrangling	B.	precursor	
	C.	feasibility	D.	apathy	

31

78. A. in accordance with   B. in spite of

C. in defiance of   D. in response to

79. A. intensified   B. passed

C. stalled   D. rectified

80. A. despite   B. given

C. by   D. during

IX. Write a short essay in English of 150-200 words as your answer to the following question:

What is the United Nations doing to address climate change?

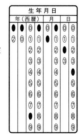

マークシート記入例

東京の本会場でA級を受験する、国連 太郎さん、受験番号が「東京01-20001」、生年月日が「1980年10月24日」の場合の記入例です。

【受験番号/氏名】
それぞれ受験票の記載通りに記入してください。

【受験地区】
受験記号・番号の、都道府県部分を塗りつぶしてください。

【会場番号】
都道府県部分に続く2桁の数字を塗りつぶしてください。

【受験番号】
ハイフン（−）以降の5桁の数字を塗りつぶしてください。

【受験級】
「A」と記入し、下段のA級部分を塗りつぶしてください。

【生年月日】
4桁の西暦・月・日を塗りつぶしてください。
10未満の月・日の十の位は、「0」を塗りつぶしてください。

※HB以上の鉛筆を用いてマークをしてください。

※他の地区から会場を変更して受験する場合でも、受験票に記載されている受験地区・会場番号をマークしてください。

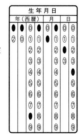

33

2019年
第1回試験

解答・解説

2019年　国連英検 A 級第 1 回試験
解答・解説

＊〔　〕内は訳出上の補足や説明

I	『わかりやすい国連の活動と世界［改訂版］』に基づき， 空所を埋めるのに最も適切なものを 4 つの選択肢の中から 1 つ選びなさい。

1.　解答：A

訳例　国連総会は 1985 年，国連創設 40 周年を祝うことを決定し，10 月 24 日の国際平和年宣言に向けて，一連の特別記念行事を開催した（『わかりやすい国連の活動と世界［改訂版］』p.30。以下，書名略）。

2.　解答：D

訳例　平和維持活動については国連憲章に明確に述べられていないが，紛争を管理しその平和的解決をはかる国際的に容認された方法として，過去 40 年以上にわたって徐々に形を成してきた（同 p.60）。

3.　解答：B

訳例　国連加盟国ないしは加盟数カ国，あるいは事務総長が平和維持活動の設置を提案する際には，3 つの基本的条件を満たさなければならない（同 p.61）。

4.　解答：C

訳例　第 30 条は，この宣言の下ではいかなる国家，団体，個人も，宣言に掲げられた「権利および自由の破壊を目的とする行為を行う，あるいは活動に参加する」権利を主張することはできない，と警告している（同 p.73）。

5.　解答：B

訳例　総会の定例会議は毎年 9 月の第 3 火曜日に始まり，12 月半ばまで続く（同 p.42）。

6.　解答：C

訳例　総会は 1974 年に世界食糧会議をローマで招集し，国際社会全体が開発および

国際経済協力の大きな流れの中で世界食糧問題の解決に取り組む方法を具体的に審議した（同 p.113）。

7. 解答：C

訳例　UNHCR の基本的な職務は，定義によれば母国の保護を受けていない難民に国際的保護を与えることである（同 p.117）。

8. 解答：A

訳例　発足時の加盟国 51 カ国は，サンフランシスコ会議に出席したが，それ以前に連合国宣言に署名し，のち国連憲章に調印，これを批准した国々である（同 p.31）。

9. 解答：C

訳例　総会は 1994 年，テロ行為はどこで，だれによって行われたかを問わず，すべて犯罪であり正当化できないものとして非難する「国際テロリズムを排除するための措置に関する宣言」を採択した（同 p.81）。

10. 解答：D

訳例　発足当初から国連は，憲章第 55 条に「より高い生活水準，完全雇用，経済的および社会的進歩と発展の条件を促進する」という誓約を掲げ，貧しい国々の開発に向けての努力を援助してきた（同 p.110）。

II　下線を引いた動詞の最も適切な変化形を 4 つの選択肢の中から 1 つ選びなさい。

11. 解答：C

解説　下線部を含む部分は〈call on＋目的語＋to 不定詞〉の形で，「～に対し…することを求める」の意味になっているので，C が正解。

12. 解答：B

解説　下線部を含む部分は〈help＋to 不定詞または原形不定詞〉の形で，「～が…する手助けをする」の意味。選択肢で該当するのは，B の原形不定詞の galvanize のみ。

37

13. 解答：A

解説 下線部直前の the country's tenth and the world's second largest とつながって意味を成すのは A のみ。

14. 解答：C

解説 下線部は意味上の主語 Ebola を伴い，前置詞 of の目的語の動名詞となるので，C が正解。

15. 解答：A

解説 下線部から predicted までが主語になり，ここではこれからの話をしているので，該当するのは A のみ。

16. 解答：D

解説 responded の直後は that 節で，下線部には the WHO ... countries を主語とし現在の状況を説明する動詞が必要。よって，D が正解。

17. 解答：D

解説 charge A with B の形で「A に B を委託する」という意味になる。意味を成し，文法的に正しいのは the Emergency Committee, charged with ..., （～を委託された緊急委員会）となる D のみ。

18. 解答：B

解説 SVO の文型で that 以下が O に，下線部が V に相当する。よって，B が正解。

19. 解答：A

解説 下線部は laws を修飾し，laws は動詞 design の意味上の目的語になるので，A が正解。

20. 解答：C

解説 It is important that ... の that 節の動詞として適切なのは仮定法現在なので，C が正解。

訳例　　公衆衛生の専門家で構成する国際団体が月曜日，世界保健機関（WHO）に対し，コンゴのエボラ出血熱大流行を「国際的〔に懸念される〕公衆衛生上の緊急事態」〔PHEIC〕として宣言することを検討するため緊急委員会の開催を要請した。

　　専門家団体は医学専門誌『ランセット』〔に投稿した論文の中〕で，そうした呼びかけが「昨年5月に始まったエボラ出血熱の大流行に対応するハイレベルの政治的，資金的，技術的支援」を促進する上で役立つだろうと述べている。

　　わずか6カ月前にコンゴ東部で宣言された今回の大流行は，記録が始まって以来コンゴでは10回目となる発生で，規模としては世界史上2番目の大きなものとなっている。武力紛争や人口密度の高さ，政情不安，集団移動も感染拡大の要因となった。

　　筆頭著者で，ジョージタウン大学オニール国内および国際保健法研究所のローレンス・ゴスティン学部長は，「流行は抑え込まれておらず，地域に拡大するリスクが高いし，世界的に広まる恐れもある」と話す。

　　この専門家らは特に，エボラ出血熱が南スーダンなど近隣諸国に拡大する懸念があると指摘。南スーダンについては，エボラ出血熱の流行を抑制する能力が非常に低く，世界でも最も脆弱な国の1つだとしている。

　　「暴力が横行し，飢饉が予想されるこの国で，この病気の蔓延を防ぐ大胆な措置をとることは，人道危機を防ぐ上で決定的に重要だ」（ゴスティン氏）。

　　専門家らは，公衆衛生上の影響や新規性，規模，人々の移動など国際的緊急事態を宣言する基準は満たされたと主張している。

　　これに対してWHOは月曜日，専門家委員会の会合が必要となる兆候がないかどうか，WHOとコンゴ国内や近隣諸国のWHO提携先で引き続き状況を監視していると述べた。

　　WHOのタリク・ヤシャレヴィチ報道官は，「もしそのような兆候が見られれば，事務局長が会議を招集する」と述べた。

　　緊急事態宣言の発令を担当する緊急委員会の第1回会合は10月17日に開催された。

　　〔今回〕注意が呼びかけられているのは，エボラ出血熱が発生から6カ月でコンゴ国内の18の保健区域に広がり，初期の流行地の多くではすでに沈静化されたものの，ここ数週間で新たな流行地域が現れたためだ。

　　ただ，専門家グループはまた，月曜日の呼びかけとは裏腹に，「国際的な公衆衛生緊急事態宣言がコンゴ国内における取引の禁止や移動制限など，悪影響を及ぼす可能性もある」と警鐘を鳴らしてもいる。このためグループはWHOと国連に対し，「この種の不当行為を防止することを目的とする法律に違反した国を指摘するなど，違法かつ有害な規制を防ぐべく積極的な措置をとる」よう求めた（ゴスティン氏による）。

緊急委員会は 10 月，「国際的な渡航制限や貿易制限を適用せず，近隣諸国が準備と監視を加速させることが特に重要である」との判断を下した。

空所を埋めるのに文法的・論理的に最もふさわしいものを
4 つの選択肢の中から 1 つ選びなさい。

21.　解答：C
解説　warned that ... and that ... のように that 節が 2 つの構文となっている。よって，C が正解。

22.　解答：D
解説　空所の直前の With only とつながって意味を成すのは D のみ。

23.　解答：C
解説　空所部分が文全体の中で意味を成すのは，分詞構文となる C。

24.　解答：A
解説　空所の直前の need to とつながって意味を成すのは A のみ。

25.　解答：A
解説　空所の直前の reminded the とつながって意味を成すのは，〈remind＋目的語＋that 節〉の構文となる A のみ。

26.　解答：D
解説　It's very の後には補語と仮主語 it を説明する表現が必要となる。それを満たしているのは D。

27.　解答：B
解説　文全体の構造を考えると，空所には動詞部分が必要。それを満たし，意味を成しているのは B のみ。

28.　解答：C
解説　空所の直後の all countries と結びついて意味を成すのは C のみ。

29.　解答：B

解説　空所の直後の decision と結びついて意味を成すのは，make some … decisions となる B のみ。

30.　解答：A

解説　全体の文構造から，To … Katowice が主語となる。この 3 人称単数の主語に適するのは，compromises と動詞に 3 単現の s がついている A のみ。

訳例　「1 週間前，私はこの会議のオープニングスピーチを行ったが，その中で……私は，気候変動が我々〔の取り組み〕よりも速いペースで進んでいること，そしてこの流れを逆転させるのに必要な場としてカトヴィツェ会議〔ポーランド〕がはっきり成功〔と言えるもの〕にならなければいけない，と注意を促した」。グテーレス事務総長はこのように述べた。

　　12 月 2 日に〔開幕した〕この会議には，これまでに気候変動対策の意思決定者や支持者，活動家ら数千人が参加しているが，その主な目的は 1 つである。それは，地球の気温上昇を産業革命前の水準比で 2℃未満——しかもなるべく 1.5℃に近い値——とすることを約束した 2015 年パリ協定の締約国 197 カ国に対して，グローバルな指針を採択することである。

　　会議の交渉期限を 3 日後に控え，グテーレス事務総長は「交渉文書では進展があったが，まだまだ問題が山積している」と遺憾の意を表明した。議論の輻輳（ふくそう）を受けて COP24 議長国のポーランドは水曜日，「交渉の新たなたたき台」となる文案を示した。

　　グテーレス氏は「主な政治課題は未解決のまま」とするとともに，「これは驚くことではない——我々はこの作業が複雑だということは認識している。ただ，時間が足りない」と注意を促し，気候変動に関する政府間パネル（IPCC）が 10 月に発表した気がかりな地球温暖化特別報告書について触れた。

　　同氏は交渉に行き詰まった各国代表団に対し，次のように述べた。「これまで 10 日間，皆さまの多くが長く苦しい作業を続けてきた。そのご尽力に感謝したい。ただ，我々がパリでした約束を守ろうと思うなら，合意を得る努力をさらに進める必要がある」。

　　事務総長は交渉担当者に対し，「低排出かつ気候変動に強い世界に向け，経済の移行を図るための予測可能かつ調達可能な資金の流れ」に関して意欲を高めるよう呼びかけた。

　　事務総長は聴衆に対し，先進国には開発途上国の努力を支援する経済面での義務があると念を押した。この義務は，パリ協定の元となる条約で，25 年以上前の 1992 年に調印された国連気候変動〔枠組〕条約（UNFCCC）に定めら

れている。

「必要な行動に対して，〔時期や規模が〕予見できるような支援が得られなか
ったことについて，気候変動の影響を受けて苦しんでいる人々に対して弁明す
ることは非常に難しい」と同氏は述べた。

グテーレス氏は，COP24 の開幕後に世界銀行や各国際開発金融機関，民間
部門などが行ったさまざまな経済〔支援〕に関する発表に歓迎の意を表した。
しかし，同氏は先進国に対し，3 年前にパリで取り決められたとおり，「拠出
金を増額し，2020 年までに総額を年間 1,000 億ドルとする」よう求めた。

グテーレス事務総長は資源を増やすことに加え，パリ協定を実施するための
「柔軟でしかも強固なルール」を策定することも要請した。これは，気候変動
条約の締約国自らによって，2018 年がこれら指針の期限の年に定められてい
たためで，各国が透明性のあるしかたで気候変動対策を進められるようにする
目的がある。

事務総長は「国によって状況も能力も環境も異なる」と述べるとともに，「す
べての国の責任を適切にバランスさせる方式」，しかも「すべての国に対して
公平で有効」な「方式を見つけなければならない」と説明した。

これを達成するため，グテーレス氏は「緩和，適応，それに資金，技術，能
力開発などの支援提供〔など〕，あらゆる面で進捗を監視し評価するための強
力な透明性の枠組み」を通じて信頼を醸成する重要性を強調した。

事務総長は，我々にはノウハウと「社会のあらゆる部門から〔生まれつつあ
る〕驚くべき機運」があると述べるとともに，「我々に必要なのは前に進もう
とする政治的な意志だ」と付言した。

「いずれも簡単でないことは理解している。一部の人たちが厳しい政治的決
断を下す必要に迫られることは理解している」と同氏は認めつつ次のように述
べた。「しかし，いまは合意〔形成〕の時だ。いまは政治的妥協を成し遂げる
時だ。さまざまな犠牲を伴うが，全体としては我々すべてに利益をもたらすこ
とになる」。

グテーレス氏は代表団や閣僚らに対し自国の優先事項を超えて，「ともに」力
を合わせて，「あらゆる面」で決意をさらに強めて「仕事を成し遂げる」よう
求め，最後に次のように述べた。「カトヴィツェ会議でこの機会を逃せば，暴
走する気候変動を食い止める最後の絶好の機会が損なわれる。それは道徳にも
とるだけでなく，自殺行為となるだろう」。

Ⅳ 以下の文章に最も適切に当てはまる語句のペアを
4 つの選択肢の中から 1 つ選びなさい。

31. 解答：C

 イギリスの EU 離脱について述べている。第 1 空所で withdrawal「離脱」

と結びつくのは C で，第 2 空所で意味を成すのも without an agreement 「合意なしで」の意味となる C。

訳例　日本とオランダ両国の首相は水曜日，英 EU 離脱がなるべく円滑に進んでほしい〔と述べるとともに〕，EU と元加盟国〔である英国〕との将来の関係に関する合意なしの離脱となることを防ぎたい〔との考え〕を明らかにした。

32.　解答：D

解説　第 1 空所で from と結びつき意味を成すのは，D。文脈から，第 2 空所に適するのも「空白を埋める」という意味になる D のみ。

訳例　外交筋や内部関係者によると，米国が国連における多国間リーダーシップや関与から身を引く傾向が強まる中で，特に中国がその空白を埋めるべく力を入れており，日本のような国は不安定な立場に置かれている。

33.　解答：A

解説　第 1 空所に適するのは，A.「に先立って」と B.「に関して」。文脈から第 2 空所に適するのは「（正当性に対する）異議申し立て」を意味する A のみ。

訳例　ベネズエラの野党指導者フアン・グアイド氏がニコラス・マドゥロ大統領率いる政権に対する異議申し立てを強める中で，軍将校らは火曜日，予定されていた人道支援物資搬送を先回りする形でコロンビア国境の橋を封鎖した。

34.　解答：A

解説　文脈から第 1 空所に適するのは A.「批准」と B.「肯定」。両者のうち第 2 空所に適するのは A.「示す」のみ。

訳例　国連のアントニオ・グテーレス事務総長は金曜日，マケドニア旧ユーゴスラビア共和国の国名変更をギリシャ議会が批准したことに祝意を表し，約 28 年にわたりこの地域を混乱に陥れてきた呼称論争に終止符を打った両国の指導者を称賛した。

35.　解答：C

解説　第 2 空所に適するのは，B.「産業の」と C.「国家の」。文脈から第 1 空所に適するのは C.「対立」のみ。

訳例　西側諸国は，中国の技術革命が突き付ける難問が，知的財産の窃盗や国家スパイ活動をめぐるファーウェイと米国との対立よりもはるかに根深いものである

ことを理解する必要がある。英スパイ最高幹部が述べた。

36. 解答：B

解説 文の前半は〈with＋O＋分詞〉の形で付帯状況を表している。第1空所には anniversary が意味上の主語になる動詞の現在分詞が入り，適しているのはBの「迫っている」。

訳例 シリアの悲惨な内戦が〔勃発から〕8周年〔となる日〕を目前に控え，新任の国連シリア特使は安全保障理事会に対し，戦争終結に向けた複雑な政治ロードマップに関する初めてのブリーフィングを行い，「公平かつ懸命に」取り組むことを約束した。

37. 解答：D

解説 文脈から第1空所に適するのはA.「反乱」，D.「反乱」の2つ。第2空所に適するのはDの「委譲した」のみ。

訳例 〔スーダンで〕木曜日，数千人が数カ所で抗議デモを行った。2カ月続くオマル・アル・バシル大統領に対する反乱の中でも最も広い範囲に及ぶもの。緊急法廷が数百人に対して夜遅くまで審理を行い，バシル大統領が与党党首としての権限を副党首に委譲したことを受けて〔行われた〕。

38. 解答：D

解説 第1空所に適するのは，B.「非難した」，D.「非難した」の2つ。C.「非難した」の目的語となるのは，悪いことに対して責任のある人や物なので適さない。文脈から第2空所に適するのは，D.「司法，裁判」のみ。

訳例 国連人権高等弁務官は，ジャンムー・カシミール州プルワマ地区で2月14日〔発生した〕インド治安部隊に対する自爆攻撃を強く非難し，責任者を裁きにかけるよう当局に求めた。

39. 解答：C

解説 第1空所に適するのは，A.「懲罰的な」とC.「報復の」。文脈から第2空所に適するのは，C.「課す」のみ。

訳例 キャタピラー社のトラック，ゼロックス社の機器，サムソナイト・インターナショナル社のスーツケースやバッグ──ドナルド・トランプ米大統領が欧州連合（EU）に対して自動車関税を課すとの脅しを押し通した場合，EUの報復関税を受けると考えられる米国製品の中に〔これらが含まれるという〕。EU高官

が明らかにした。

40. 解答：A

解説 第2空所に適するのはAの「よい結果を導くような」，B.「好都合な」，C.「確実な」。第1空所に適するのはA.「騒乱，混乱」のみ。

訳例 ニカラグア政府は政治的・社会的混乱を解決したいとしているが，反対派に対する逮捕，有罪判決が続き，「誠実で包括的な対話」を導く環境整備が明らかに妨げられている。国連人権高等弁務官が金曜日，このように発言した。

V 文法的，語法的にふさわしくないものを下線の中から1つ選びなさい。

41. 解答：B

解説 larger than → more than。文構造から動詞 tripled を修飾する副詞句 more than を使う。

訳例 国連は水曜日，アフガニスタンにおける地雷その他の爆発物による死傷者の数が2012年以降3倍以上に増加したことを明らかにし，生存者に対してより長期的な支援を提供するよう求める呼びかけを支持した。

42. 解答：D

解説 wound → wounded。wound は dead との対で，〈leave＋O＋過去分詞〉の形になるので，wounded とすべき。

訳例 国連事務総長は土曜日，米ピッツバーグのシナゴーグで死者を出した銃乱射事件に「大きなショックを受けている」と述べた。事件では11人が死亡したほか，数人が負傷し，一部は重傷と報じられている。

43. 解答：A

解説 withdraw → withdraw from。withdraw は自動詞として使われているので，前置詞の from が必要。

訳例 日本は，30年ぶりの商業捕鯨再開に向け国際捕鯨委員会からの脱退を決めた。複数の政府関係者が火曜日，明らかにした。

44. 解答：C

解説 of → 不要。despite は前置詞なので，of は不要。

訳例 2018年の首都圏への転入者が転出者を上回る〔転入超過〕が14万人近くに

45

達したことが木曜日，政府の報告で明らかになった。2020 年までにこの流れ
を逆転させ，地方創生を目指す安倍晋三首相の方針に逆行する〔形だ〕。

45. 解答：D

解説 which → whose。文意から assemblies は municipalities に属している
ものなので，whose が適切。

訳例 沖縄県の玉城デニー知事は，米軍の主要な飛行場〔普天間飛行場〕の移設問題
をめぐる県民投票について，関連予算〔案〕が議会で可決されていない 5 つの
自治体が参加しない場合でも，予定どおり 2 月 24 日に実施する意向を明らか
にした。

46. 解答：A

解説 to hold → holding。consider が目的語に取るのは動名詞のみ。

訳例 日本海の呼称問題をめぐり，日本は韓国や他の国々との非公式協議を検討して
いる。政府高官が示唆した。日韓の一連の外交摩擦のまた新たな〔段階〕とな
るかもしれない。

47. 解答：A

解説 are stepping up → are being stepped up。文意から efforts は step up
の目的語となるので，受動態の進行形とするべき。

訳例 インドネシアのスマトラ島〔南〕端部とジャワ島〔西〕端部では，スンダ海峡
沿いの人口密集地に土曜夜，津波が押し寄せたことを受け，政府主導の救援活
動が強化されている。

48. 解答：B

解説 urgent → urgently。文構造から動詞 offer を修飾するので，副詞の
urgently とすべき。

訳例 国連難民高等弁務官事務所（UNHCR）は 2018 年の末日に当たり，地中海の
救助船に乗り込んでいる幼児を含む難民・移民 49 人について，安全に上陸で
きる港を緊急に提供するよう国連加盟国に求めた。

49. 解答：D

解説 raise → rise。raise は給与などの「昇給」，気持の「高まり」という意味
で使う。ここでは temperature（気温）に対して使う「上昇」という意

味の rise にすべき。

訳例　国連支援により作成された新たな報告書が月曜日に発表された〔が,〕その調査結果からオゾン層の回復が続いていることが分かった。グローバルな合意によってどういうことが達成できるかを実証するものであり, また, 地球の気温の急激な上昇を食い止める, より積極的な気候変動対策を促すものとして高く評価されている。

50.　解答：B

解説　is → are。主語が options と複数形なので, be 動詞は are となる。

訳例　4月1日に発表される新元号について, 従来の元号が漢籍を典拠とするものが多い中で, 今回の候補名の中には国書から採った案があるとみられる。複数の政府関係者が明らかにした。

VI	以下の文章の中に含まれる太字の語句および空所の意味として 文脈上最も近いものを4つの選択肢の中から1つ選びなさい。

51.　解答：D

解説　faltered は「よろめいた」の意。最も意味が近いのは D.「激しく揺れた」。

52.　解答：B

解説　into の後には好ましくない状態が示されているので, 空所に最も適するのは, degenerating into で「〜（という状態）に悪化すること」という意味になる B。

53.　解答：D

解説　bailed out は「〜を救済した」の意。意味が最も近いのは D.「〜を支えた, 〜の後ろ盾になった」。

54.　解答：A

解説　空所の直前では金融危機の際のアメリカと英国の状況について述べている。空所の後ではそうした状況の中で浮上した見方を説明している。両者をつなぐのは A.「それゆえ」。

55. 解答：B

解説 coming up with < come up with は「考え出す」の意。意味が最も近いのは B の原形「考案する」。

56. 解答：A

解説 dissipated は「消散した」の意。最も意味が近いのは A.「激減した」。

57. 解答：C

解説 splintered は「バラバラになった」の意。最も意味が近いのは C.「断片化した」。

58. 解答：D

解説 mobilise はここでは「集めて何かをさせる」の意。最も意味が近いのは D.「何かをするよう駆り立てる」。A にも B にも「集める」の意味はあるが，A は「集めてまとめる」，B は「会議などを招集する」の意味。また C にも「駆り立てる」という意味はあるが，「暴動や戦争に駆り立てる，扇動する」という意味になってしまう。

59. 解答：A

解説 touch a nerve は「神経を逆なでする，激しい苛立ちを引き起こす」の意。最も意味が近いのは A.「（激しい反応を引き起こすような）厄介な話題を反映している」。

60. 解答：D

解説 ここでは政治家の選挙活動について述べていて，空所の動詞の目的語は「一般の人々の支持」。この文脈に最も適する動詞は D.「集める，結集する」。

訳例 今日の世界には，民衆が政治変革を求める例が数多く見られる。〔そうした事態は〕通常，政治家が約束を守れないように思われたときに発生する。例えば，2008 年を見てみよう。アマルティア・セン（2009）が「危機の年」と呼んだ年である。原油価格の急騰が世界的な燃料・石油製品価格の高騰を招き，2008 年秋には米国の経済危機が急速に拡大して以前からの問題を悪化させ，

世界経済が低迷した。

　米国は，国民が政治に全面的に参加することを認めている国である。国民が集団として選挙に参加することで国が進むべき方向を決める場所である。「自由な人間の国」，「誰でも大統領になれる」というスローガンが思い浮かぶ。しかしその米国も，他の多くの似かよった政治体制と同様，富める者を優遇するシステムへの劣化〔という問題〕に直面している。現在の米国では，国民所得全体の21％を国民の上位1％が得ており，この比率は時とともに悪化している。1970年代には，上位1％の所得比率は「わずか」10％程度であった。この問題は2008年金融危機の後に深刻化した。この危機によって，米国社会の格差の程度と，大多数の国民が感じていた，公共政策に対する自分たちの影響力の欠如が露呈したのである（ピケティ2014を参照）。米国人200万人が家を失ったいわゆる「サブプライム住宅ローン」の破綻は，その後さらに金融システム全体に影響を及ぼす，より大きな危機へと発展した。米国政府は，金融システム全体の崩壊を防ぐため，一部の大企業と銀行を数千億ドル規模で救済した。これに加えて緊縮財政政策〔が実施され〕，経済恐慌に伴う政府の財源不足により給付金や公共サービスが削減された。この一般的なパターンはイギリスなど，他の自由主義経済国にも見られた。そのため一部の人々の間に，政府が最富裕層には金を与え，最貧困層からは金を取ったという見方が浮上してきた。「占拠せよ」運動は，この認知された事態に対する，大きな広がりと多様性を持つ反応であった。政党，選挙，ロビー活動といった民主的な政治と統治の伝統的な手段に効果がないことへの反動であった。

　「占拠せよ」運動は，米国金融業界のメッカであるウォール街を「不労で得た」特権と富の象徴と見て，これに抗議したのである——緊縮政策による削減を考え，実施していたのは政治家であったのだが……。この運動は2011年9月17日，ウォール街近くのズコッティ公園で始まった。批判する側からは，活動家らが要求の内容を明確にしていないことや，不満だけを強調しがちであることが指摘された。しかし，次のような明確な価値観の体系が確実に現れた。すなわち，連帯——社会の各機関は相互利益を最大化することを目指すべき。多様性——差し迫った問題に対する多様な解決策。公正——解決策と分配の面における〔公正〕。管理——特に自己管理，自由，自律。

　「占拠せよ」運動の発生に続いて，同様の占拠が世界中で何百件も——といっても米国と西欧が中心だが——起きた。あれから数年を経たいまも，抗議行動の引き金となった問題が解決していないことは明らかである。しかし，運動からはエネルギーがほとんど失われてしまった。その1つの理由は，行動への明確な道筋の提示を可能にするような共通の土台を抗議者らが作り上げ，明確に示すことができなかったためである（政党や革命運動であればそれが優先事項となっていただろう）。その代わりに抗議の人々は，「我々は99％」というスローガンを生み出し，1970年代に始まる格差の拡大によって女性や若者，

マイノリティーが割りを食っていることを強調してみせただけであった。占拠運動は，2011 年 11 月にニューヨーク市長が抗議運動を排除する決定を下したことを受けて分裂し，指導者も具体的な要求もなしに，世界のあらゆる「間違った」ことに対する，焦点のぼやけた抗議運動となった。

　占拠運動による社会批判は多くの人々の共感を呼んでいるが，目標を達成する現実的で達成可能な手段を提示しているかどうかは疑問である。民衆を動かして貧困を軽減する最善の方法は何か？　多くの人々は，貧困の軽減を目指す取り組み（たとえば，公営住宅の建設や食料配給券の削減防止など）には，政治の主流部分が関与することが必要だと主張するだろう。批判する側は，「改革志向の政府が貧しい人々を引き上げて差別を緩和する」という革新の理想を新世代の活動家らが忘れ，放棄し，看過していると言っている。はっきりしているのは，米国や他の西側諸国における経済的・社会的構造の組織的分断をめぐる懸念に対して，「占拠せよ」運動が発言権を与えたということである。これらの懸念は，いまも鎮まらない神経を刺激する〔かのごとくである〕——香港における雨傘革命後の状況とよく似かよっている。また，やはり香港と同様，一部の政治指導者や警察幹部が示した拒否反応に権力者の偽善を感じた人もいた。2008 年以降，米国では，選挙活動中の政治家が多くの人々の支持を得る手段として，ウォール街〔大企業〕支持よりは「メインストリート」〔地方の中小企業〕支持を打ち出すことがいまではふつうになっている。

 VII 下線部の単語や句の意味を最もよく表しているものを
4 つの選択肢の中から 1 つ選びなさい。

61.　解答：B

解説　原形 unveil は「発表する」の意。その意味を最もよく表しているのは，
B.「紹介する」。

62.　解答：C

解説　原形 track はここでは「監視する，見守る」の意。その意味を最もよく
表しているのは，C.「見守る，常に把握する」。

63.　解答：D

解説　duration は「持続時間」の意。その意味を最もよく表しているのは，
D.「時間の長さ」。

64. 解答：A

解説 下線部は「実際のところ確かなものは何もない」の意。それを最もよく説明しているのは A.「明確な証拠を示すことができない」。

65. 解答：D

解説 下線部は「その先に」の意。その意味を最もよく表しているのは，D.「将来に」。

66. 解答：A

解説 tackle は「取り組む」の意。その意味を最もよく表しているのは，A.「挑む」。

67. 解答：B

解説 下線部は「次のように考えてみてほしい」の意。その意味を最もよく表しているのは，B.「あなたが次のようなことをしていると想像してほしい」。

68. 解答：D

解説 significantly は「著しく」の意。その意味を最もよく表しているのは，D.「明らかにわかるほど」。

69. 解答：B

解説 measures は「対策」の意。その意味を最もよく表しているのは，B.「（計画などの）実行」。

70. 解答：C

解説 下線部は「～であると考えれば」の意。その意味を最もよく表しているのは，C.「～ということであるから」。

訳例　国連の保健専門家らは火曜日，年齢 12 歳から 35 歳で，スマートフォンの音楽再生など大きな音にさらされることで不治の難聴となるリスクを抱える人が世界で 10 億人以上に及ぶと述べるとともに，この問題に取り組むための新しいガイドラインを発表した。

騒音性難聴や耳鳴り（耳の内部で音が鳴るのがよく〔見られる症状〕）などの関連症状予防のために出された今回の勧告には，音楽を聴く音量と時間を監視できるよう，個人用オーディオ機器の機能を高めることも含まれている。

世界保健機関（WHO）と国際電気通信連合（ITU）によるセーフリスニング機器およびシステムに関する新規格では，個人用オーディオ機器に「音の許容限度」機能を搭載することを勧告している。ユーザーが音声や音楽に触れる音量や時間を追跡するソフトウェアだ。

WHOで技官として聴力喪失と難聴の予防に取り組むシェリー・チャーダ博士は，「オーディオ機器からヘッドフォンでしょっちゅう音楽を聴く。〔そういう〕自分が大好きなことをしているだけでも，度を越せば難聴になる。そのリスクを抱えている若者が〔世界に〕10億人以上もいる」と述べた。

「現時点では，この〔聴き方〕でいいのか，それともこのままいくと数年後には耳鳴症や難聴になるものなのか，判断する確かな手がかりは直感以外にない」。

世界的に普及が続くスマートフォンなどの個人用オーディオ機器を危険な音量で聴いている若者が約半数にのぼることを示すデータもある中，WHOとITUが共同で進めるこのイニシアチブは，どういう場合が過度の騒音となるかという認識が不足している問題に取り組む試みだ。

WHOによると，現在，難聴を放置することで世界経済にもたらされるコストは7億5,000万ドルと推定される。

チャーダ博士は次のように説明する。「幹線道路をスピードメーターや制限速度なしに走るようなものだと思ってほしい。我々が今回提案したのは，スマートフォンにスピードメーターが搭載されるということ。その測定システムによって，どのくらいの量の音を聞いているかが分かり，限界を超えた場合に教えてもらえる〔ようにする〕ということだ」。

さらに，国連による産業界への勧告には，保護者が音量を調節する機能も盛り込まれ，〔規格を策定する〕2年間の議論には，政府，消費者団体，市民社会などからの専門家と並んで産業界も参加した。

このガイドラインではまた，ユーザーによるオーディオ機器使用量を監視してユーザーごとのリスナープロファイルを作成し，ユーザーの聴き方がどの程度安全か（あるいは安全でないか）を知らせる機能を，技術を使って実現することを提案している。

チャーダ博士はこう説明する。「我々の提案は，音量の自動制限，自動低減，保護者による音量調節〔機能〕だ。音の限界値を超えた場合に，耳を傷めないようなレベルまで音量を自動的に下げる機能を選べるようにすることだ」。

WHOによると，〔世界人口の〕20人に1人より多い割合で（大人4億3,200万人，子供3,400万人）重度の難聴があり，生活の質に影響が及んでいる。

同じくWHOによれば，聴覚障害者の大部分は貧困国や中所得国に住んでお

り，2050年までに9億人以上が聴力を著しく損なうとみられる。

WHOでは，難聴者の約半数は公衆衛生対策によって予防できるとしている。今回の勧告は3月3日（日）の「世界耳の日」を控えて発表された。

WHOのテドロス・アダノム・ゲブレイェスス事務局長は次のように述べた。「難聴を予防する技術的なノウハウはあるのだから，これほどたくさんの若者が音楽を聴いて聴力を損なう状態が続くことはあってはならない。聴力は失うと，もとには戻らないことを若者たちに知ってほしい」。

| **VIII** | 文脈上，空所を埋めるのに最もふさわしいものを 4つの選択肢の中から1つ選びなさい。 |

71. 解答：B

解説 空所にはマドゥロ大統領政権を説明する語が入る。主語のグアイド氏はその終焉（しゅうえん）を早めようと動いていて，第5パラグラフでは現政権をdictatorship（独裁政治）と表現している。よって，ふさわしいのはB.「独裁的な」。

72. 解答：A

解説 空所に入るのは，the amnesty（恩赦）を主語とする動詞。選択肢の中でふさわしいのは，A.「棚上げになっている」。

73. 解答：C

解説 空所の直前の文では「マドゥロ政権に対して，政敵のグアイド氏に直接行動を起こさないよう，米国が脅している」と，直後では「政権が反体制側に対して弾圧を行っている」と，それぞれ述べている。両者をつなぐのにふさわしいのは，C.「それにもかかわらず」。

74. 解答：B

解説 空所の後には過去の出来事，空所の前にはそれに基づいた予測が述べられているので，B.「〜の後に」がふさわしい。

75. 解答：A

解説 空所にはHe（グアイド氏）を主語としanother concern（もう1つの懸念）を目的語とする動詞が入り，直後ではその懸念について述べてい

る。よって，A.「表明した」がふさわしい。

76. 解答：C

解説 文脈に沿い，raise the と結びつくのは，raise the stakes（賭け金を上げる，危険度を高める）のコロケーションとなる C.「賭け金」。

77. 解答：B

解説 「食料や医薬品を国内に運び込む動きを，侵略の _____ とするマドゥロ政権の警告」と述べているので，空所にふさわしいのは B.「前触れ」。

78. 解答：D

解説 「トランプ政権がマドゥロ政権の〜（といった行為）_____，治安部隊員 6 人に制裁措置を科した」と述べているので，空所にふさわしいのは D.「〜に対して」。

79. 解答：C

解説 空所に入るのは a bill（法案）を主語とする動詞で，空所の直後では「寛大すぎるとする強硬派議員の反発を買い，グアイド氏自身が議長を務める当の国民議会で」と述べているので，ふさわしいのは C.「行き詰まった」。

80. 解答：A

解説 「我々は，命が脅威にさらされること _____ ベネズエラの街区を占拠し続ける」と述べているので，A.「〜があったとしても，〜にもかかわらず」がふさわしい。

訳例 　先週ベネズエラを出国した〔野党指導者〕，フアン・グアイド氏が最初に訪問したのはコロンビアだった。しかし，独裁的なニコラス・マドゥロ大統領政権の終 焉（しゅうえん）を早めるため，食料と医薬品を越境して搬入する〔目論見〕は失敗に終わり，その後ブラジルへ向かった。
　同氏はパラグアイでの会合後，金曜日にアルゼンチン入り。そしてきょうはエクアドルへ向かっており，そこでレニン・モレノ大統領の歓迎を受ける。ペルーのマルティン・ビスカラ大統領も，副外相の話によると，グアイド氏にリマ訪問を要請したという。

　同氏はまもなく帰国するとはいうものの，近隣諸国歴訪が長引くにつれて，いつ，どのようにしてカラカスに戻るつもりなのかという疑問の声が上がっている。グアイド氏は野党が多数を占める国民議会の議長であり，ベネズエラへの再入国を阻まれることはおろか，外国渡航禁止令違反で投獄されるリスクも抱えている。一方，自分の側に付く軍人らに対して約束した恩赦は議会内で棚上げにされており，また，再燃した街頭抗議活動は焦点がぼやけてしまった。

　米国は，他の50余りの国々とともにグアイド氏を不正選挙後のベネズエラの正当な指導者として承認しており，マドゥロ〔大統領〕がこの最大のライバルに対して直接行動を起こせば甚大な影響が生じるだろうとして脅している。にもかかわらず，ベネズエラの社会主義政権派はすでに反体制派を追放し，数百人を投獄した。

　グアイド氏は35歳の国会議員。今回の歴訪は同盟国との結びつきを深め，独裁政権を倒す計画を練るためと話す。だが，ベネズエラへの人道支援物資搬入が先週，力で阻止されただけに，国外滞在が長引くほど，同氏が率いるマドゥロ打倒の運動は勢いを失う公算が高くなる。

　「我々はこれからすぐにカラカスに戻り，ベネズエラ全国民のために誓った仕事を続ける」。同氏は〔パラグアイの〕マリオ・アブド・ベニテス大統領と非公開会談を行った後，〔首都〕アスンシオンでこのように述べた。

　金曜日，グアイド氏はさらにアルゼンチンに飛び，マウリシオ・マクリ大統領に迎えられた。約30分にわたる同大統領との会談後，グアイド氏は数日中に帰国すると重ねて述べるとともに，国民議会が土曜日にも政府に対する抗議の日程を発表することを明らかにした。同氏はまた別の懸念も表明した。

　「ベネズエラへの介入はピザの配達とは違う。大きな責任を伴う。誰も力の行使は望んでいない」。

　カラカスの世論調査会社デルフォスのフェリックス・セイハス社長によると，グアイド氏は刑務所に入れられた場合に考えられる影響を分析しているが，政府も同氏を投獄した場合の影響を検討しているという。

　「政府にとって最良のシナリオは，グアイド氏が戻らないことだ」とセイハス氏は話す。同盟国を歴訪することで，「グアイド氏は投獄される可能性を高めようとしている」。

　グアイド氏は土曜日，通信社〔ニュースウェブサイト〕インフォバエの取材に応じ，同氏がベネズエラで逮捕されることになれば「民衆蜂起」につながるだろうと語った。

　だが，反対派は先週の土曜日を，飢えに苦しむベネズエラへの支援物資搬入によりマドゥロ政権を打倒する日としてすでに宣伝していた。しかし，いまだ〔政府に〕忠誠を誓う警察や軍部は，国境の検問所に備蓄されている食料や医薬品を移動させようとした数千人もの活動家らを追い払った。この動きを侵略の前触れとしたマドゥロ政権の警告に従ったのだ。

催涙ガスやプラスチックペレット弾，弾丸などを一斉に発射。少なくとも4人が死亡，数百人が負傷し，グアイド氏は国外に足止めとなった。金曜日，トランプ政権は「非難すべき暴力が行われ，悲惨な死者が出たこと，そして病気や飢えに苦しむベネズエラ人に送られるはずの食料と医薬品が不当に焼き払われたことに対し」，治安部隊員6人に制裁措置を科した。スティーヴン・ムヌーチン〔米〕財務長官が声明で発表した。

土曜日以降，治安部隊員500人以上がコロンビアへ脱走したが，部隊を率いる高級将校は1人も寝返っていない。問題をいっそう複雑にしているのは，軍関係者が汚職や人権侵害を犯していてもグアイド氏側についた場合は恩赦を与えるという法案〔だ〕。これを寛大すぎるとする強硬派議員の反発を買い，グアイド氏自身〔が議長を務める〕当の国民議会で審議が行き詰まってしまった。

グアイド氏の外遊中，ベネズエラ政府は謝肉祭休暇を延長し，国民に対して都市部を離れて海辺へ〔出かけるよう〕促した。一方，グアイド氏は「帰国後は支持者を集め，再度の抗議行動〔の計画〕を発表する」と約束している。

「我々は，命の危険を顧みることなくベネズエラの街区を占拠し続ける」。同氏はアスンシオンでこのように述べた。

IX 以下の質問に対し，150〜200語の短いエッセイを英語で書きなさい。

質問文：「国連は気候変動の対策として，どのようなことを行っているか？」

解答例 I will focus on the World Meteorological Organization (WMO) to discuss ways the UN addresses climate change.

The International Meteorological Organization (IMO), formed in 1878, became an intergovernmental association, the World Meteorological Organization, in 1939. The WMO, in 1950, became a UN specialized agency, continuing to maintain and advance knowledge on global air and water conditions. Ongoing weather variation measurements, understood as climate change, give climate models scientific foundation.

The WMO's second role in addressing climate change—reporting— considers the impacts of weather trends. Flooding, desertification, or other environmental disasters cause food insecurity and disease in affected areas, and migration to escape the tragedies. Key agencies—

UNICEF, UNHCR, UNDP, and WFP—provide humanitarian aid; WMO efforts develop preventative measures based on predictive models.

WMO reports perform another role—proposing regulations—facilitating international accords to mitigate and reverse damages human and other factors cause to the environment. These include the 1987 Montreal Protocol banning chlorofluorocarbons (CFCs), which reversed ozone layer damage, and measures detailed in the 1992 Kyoto Protocol, 2015 Paris Agreement, and December 2018 COP21.

The UN, through the work of the WMO, addresses climate change by drawing on over 140 years of scientific research, reportage, and clear action plans.

解説　全体を通しては，国連システムと現在の状況についての正確な知識を織り交ぜつつ，文章を展開するとよい。

第1パラグラフでは，与えられた質問に対して「世界気象機関（WMO）に焦点を当てて論じる」と述べている。

第2パラグラフでは，WMO 設立までの経緯を述べ，WMO の1つ目の役割が「世界の大気と水の状態に関する知識の維持と向上」であり，気象変化の測定が気候変動対策において科学的に寄与しているとしている。

第3パラグラフでは，WMO の2つ目の役割が，自然災害やそれに伴う食料不安，病気，難民といった気候変動が引き起こす影響のレポートを公表し，予測に基づく予防対策を進めることであると述べている。

第4パラグラフでは，WMO のレポートが果たすもう1つの役割に規制の提案があり，それによって，環境被害を軽減し修復する国際協定が推進されているとしている。

最後の第5パラグラフでは，国連が140年以上の実績を持つWMO の活動を通じて，気候変動対策に取り組んでいると，締めくくっている。

訳例　世界気象機関（WMO）を中心に，国連の気候変動への対応を考える。

1878年に設立された国際気象機関（IMO）は1939年，政府間機関の世界気象機関となった。WMO は1950年，国連の専門機関となり，世界の大気と水の状態に関する知識の維持と向上を図る取り組みを続けた。現在進行中の気象変化に関する測定は，気候変動〔を示す〕と考えられており，気候モデルに科学的根拠を与えるものである。

気候変動対応でWMO が果たすもう1つの役割，つまり報告においては，気

象の傾向が及ぼすさまざまな影響について検討している。洪水や砂漠化などの環境災害〔が起きると〕，被災地では食料不安や病気が発生するほか，被害から逃れるため移住が行われる。主要機関であるユニセフ，UNHCR，UNDP，WFP が人道支援を実施するのに対して，WMO の取り組みは予測モデルに基づく予防対策を進めるものである。

WMO 報告書にはもう 1 つ，規制の提案という役割があり，これによって人為その他の要因が環境に及ぼす損害を軽減・修復するための国際協定〔の取り組み〕を推進している。これには，オゾン層破壊を逆転させた 1987 年のモントリオール議定書（フロン禁止）のほか，1992 年の京都議定書，2015 年のパリ協定，2018 年 12 月の COP21 で詳述されている措置も含まれる。

国連は WMO の活動を通じ，科学研究，報道，明確な行動計画など 140 年以上におよぶ実績を生かして気候変動に対する取り組みを進めているのである。

2019 年 A 級第 1 回試験　正解一覧

I
1. A　2. D　3. B　4. C　5. B　6. C　7. C　8. A　9. C　10. D

II
11. C　12. B　13. A　14. C　15. A　16. D　17. D　18. B　19. A　20. C

III
21. C　22. D　23. C　24. A　25. A　26. D　27. B　28. C　29. B　30. A

IV
31. C　32. D　33. A　34. A　35. C　36. B　37. D　38. D　39. C　40. A

V
41. B　42. D　43. A　44. C　45. D　46. A　47. A　48. B　49. D　50. B

VI
51. D　52. B　53. D　54. A　55. B　56. A　57. C　58. D　59. A　60. D

VII
61. B　62. C　63. D　64. A　65. D　66. A　67. B　68. D　69. B　70. C

VIII
71. B　72. A　73. C　74. B　75. A　76. C　77. B　78. D　79. C　80. A

2019年
第2回試験
問題

A級

外務省後援

２０１９年度第２回国際連合公用語

英語検定試験 (120分)

受験上の注意

1. 問題用紙は試験開始の合図があるまで開いてはいけません。その間に、この**受験上の注意**を熟読しておいてください。

2. **受験番号と氏名を解答用紙（マークシートと作文用紙）に記入してください。**

3. 解答用紙の配布は１人１部のみです。複数の配布は致しません。

4. 試験開始前は、答案への解答記入は禁止です。

5. マークシートの記入は、１〜100までの記入箇所がありますが、この級では１〜80までを使います。

6. マークシートの記入は、必ずＨＢ以上の濃い鉛筆を使って該当箇所を黒く塗りつぶしてください。書き間違いの場合は「アト」が残らないように消してください。マークシートは絶対に折ったり曲げたりしないでください。

7. 受験級、受験地区、会場番号、受験番号のマークシートへの記入は監督者の指示に従い、間違いなく記入してください。**（裏表紙の「マークシート記入例」参照）**

8. 作文は、⑴読みやすい文字をペン、ボールペンまたはＨＢ以上の濃い鉛筆で書いてください。⑵使用語数の150〜200語を目安にしてください。

9. 試験問題についての質問は、印刷が不鮮明な場合を除き、一切受けつけません。

10. 中途退室の際は、マークシートと作文用紙を持って監督者に渡し、他の受験者の迷惑にならないように静かに退室してください。中途退室後の再入室はできません。

11. 試験中は他の受験者の妨げとなる行動を慎んでください。また携帯電話等の電源はお切りください。

12. マークシートと作文用紙は監督者に提出し、問題用紙はご自由にお持ち帰りください。

＊試験問題の複製や転載、インターネットへのアップロード等、いかなる媒体への転用を禁止します。

試験結果について

1. 第１次試験の結果は2019年11月27日㈬頃に受験申込書に記載された住所に郵送で通知します。

2. その間に住所変更をされた方は、郵便局へ住所変更の届け出を忘れずに行ってください。

3. 発表前の試験結果のお問合せには応じられません。

第２次試験について

1. 第１次試験合格者には、試験結果発表と同時に試験日時、会場を指定して通知します。（第１次試験を特別会場で受験した合格者には最寄りの２次試験会場が指定されます。）

2. 第２次試験は2019年12月15日㈰です。Ａ級の試験地は札幌・仙台・東京・名古屋・大阪・福岡・鹿児島・沖縄のいずれかになります。（特Ａ級との併願で特Ａ級の第１次試験に合格された方の試験地は東京と大阪になります。）あらかじめご了承願います。

公　益
財団法人 日本国際連合協会

http://www.unaj.or.jp/

I．**Fill in each of the following blanks with the most appropriate of the four alternatives according to the knowledge and information gained from Today's Guide to the United Nations.**

1. The General Assembly meets once a year in regular session, commencing on the third Tuesday in September and continuing until mid-_____. The regular session may sometimes be resumed again the following year.

2019年
第2回
問題

    A. October　　　　　　　　　　B.　November
    C. December　　　　　　　　　　D.　January

2. The Economic and Social Council (ECOSOC), which operates under the authority of the _____ , coordinates the economic and social work of the United Nations and its specialized agencies.

    A. General Assembly　　　　　　B.　International Monetary Fund
    C. Security Counsel　　　　　　　D.　World Trade Organization

3. Each member of the Security Council has one vote. Decisions on matters of procedure require the approval of at least nine of the _____ members.

    A. 12　　　　　　　　　　　　　B.　13
    C. 14　　　　　　　　　　　　　D.　15

4. The _____ United Nations Convention on the Law of the Sea is generally acclaimed as one of the most outstanding achievements of the United Nations. It established a comprehensive set of rules to govern virtually all uses of the ocean, including navigation, fisheries, mineral resource development and scientific research.

    A. 1981　　　　　　　　　　　　B.　1982
    C. 1983　　　　　　　　　　　　D.　1984

5. The regular program budget of the United Nations is approved by the General Assembly _____ .

    A. biennially　　　　　　　　　　B.　every three years
    C. every six months　　　　　　　D.　annually

6. The basic function of _____ is to extend international protection to refugees who, by definition, do not enjoy the protection of their former home country.

    A. UNV　　　　　　　　　　　　B.　WHO
    C. UNICEF　　　　　　　　　　　D.　UNHCR

7. The International Court of Justice consists of 15 judges elected by the General Assembly and the Security Council, voting independently. They are chosen on the basis of their _____ , not on the basis of nationality...
    A. commitment   B. eligibility
    C. expertise   D. qualifications

8. The name "United Nations" was suggested by United States President Franklin D. Roosevelt. It was first used officially in 1942, when representatives of _____ countries signed the Declaration by the United Nations, pledging their cooperation in the "struggle for victory over Hitlerism."
    A. 24   B. 25
    C. 26   D. 27

9. The 51 original members of the United Nations were the States that took part in the _____ Conference or had previously signed the Declaration by the United Nations, which signed and ratified the charter.
    A. Cairo   B. Yalta
    C. San Francisco   D. Potsdam

10. The Assembly proclaimed the Declaration as "a common _____ of achievement for all peoples and all nations."
    A. ground   B. basis
    C. recognition   D. standard

Ⅱ. Choose from among the four alternatives the one that is the most appropriate form of each of the underlined verbs.

British Prime Minister Theresa May and the two men (**11**) **compete** to succeed her condemned U.S. President Donald Trump's berating of four female lawmakers of color but stopped short Monday of calling his remarks racist.

Trump tweeted Sunday that the liberal Democrats should go back to the "broken and crime infested" countries they came from. All four are American citizens and three were born in the United States.

May, who is set to step down next week following her resignation over Brexit, (**12**) **think** "the language which was used to refer to the women was completely unacceptable," spokesman James Slack said.

Boris Johnson and Foreign Secretary Jeremy Hunt, the two politicians in the runoff (**13**) **replace** May as Conservative Party leader and U.K. prime minister, agreed.

Johnson said Trump's remarks were "totally unacceptable in a modern multiracial country."

"If you are the leader of a great multiracial, multicultural society, you simply cannot use that kind of language about sending people back to where they came from," he said during a debate with Hunt.

His political rival echoed the sentiment.

"I have three half-Chinese children," said Hunt, whose wife is Chinese. "And if anyone ever (**14**) **say** to them, 'Go back to China,' I would be utterly appalled."

But Hunt — who as foreign secretary is Britain's top diplomat — balked when (**15**) **ask** whether he would call Trump's comments racist, instead noting that the United States is Britain's closest ally.

"It is not going to help the situation (**16**) **use** that kind of language about the president of the United States," he said.

Johnson declined to answer when he also was asked if Trump's words (**17**) **be** racist.

The comments come at a testy time for U.K.-U.S. relations. The trans-Atlantic relationship (**18**) **rattle** in the last two weeks by the Mail on Sunday newspaper's publication of leaked diplomatic cables from Britain's ambassador in Washington criticizing the Trump administration.

Trump responded by calling Ambassador Kim Darroch "very stupid" on Twitter and (**19**) **cold-shoulder** him. Darroch resigned, saying he could no longer do his job.

Trump defended his tweets about the congresswomen, taking to Twitter again Monday (**20**) **demand** apologies from the four Democrats and claiming "so many people are angry at them and & their horrible & disgusting actions."

11. 　　A.　are competing 　　　　 B.　competing
　　　　C.　competed 　　　　　　　 D.　to compete

65

| 12. | A. | thought | B. | thinking |
| | C. | to think | D. | thinks |

| 13. | A. | to replace | B. | are replacing |
| | C. | replacing | D. | will replace |

| 14. | A. | saying | B. | said |
| | C. | has said | D. | will say |

| 15. | A. | he asked | B. | asked |
| | C. | asking | D. | to ask |

| 16. | A. | of using | B. | to use |
| | C. | in which using | D. | use |

| 17. | A. | were | B. | will be |
| | C. | has been | D. | being |

| 18. | A. | rattling | B. | has rattled |
| | C. | was rattled | D. | has been rattled |

| 19. | A. | cold-shouldering | B. | was cold-shouldered |
| | C. | cold-shouldered | D. | who cold-shouldered |

| 20. | A. | is demanding | B. | and demanded |
| | C. | to demand | D. | demanded |

Ⅲ. **Fill in each of the following blanks with the most grammatically and logically appropriate of the four alternatives.**

In an innovative partnership, the United Nations Children's Fund (UNICEF) and a Colombian social enterprise announced on Monday that **(21)** _____ _____ convert plastic waste collected in Côte d'Ivoire into modular plastic bricks. The easy-to-assemble, durable, low-cost bricks will be used to build much-needed classrooms in the West African country.

"This factory will be at the cutting edge of smart, scalable **(22)** _____ _____ Africa's children and communities face," said UNICEF Executive Director Henrietta Fore. "Its potential is threefold: more **(23)** __ _____ in the environment, and additional income avenues for the most vulnerable families."

Côte d'Ivoire needs 15,000 classrooms to meet the needs of children without a place to learn. To help fill this gap, UNICEF has partnered with Conceptos Plasticos to use **(24)** _____ Abidjan to build 500 classrooms for more than 25,000 children with the most urgent need in the next two years, with potential to increase production beyond.

"One of the major challenges facing Ivorian school children is a lack of classrooms. They either don't exist, or when they do, they are overcrowded, making learning a challenging and unpleasant experience," said UNICEF Representative Dr. Aboubacar Kampo, who **(25)** _____ . "In certain areas, for the firsttime, kindergartners from poor neighborhoods would be able to attend classrooms with less than 100 other students. Children who never thought there would be a place for them at school will be able to learn and thrive in a new and clean classroom."

More than 280 tonnes of plastic waste are produced every day in Abidjan alone. Only about five per cent is recycled — the rest mostly ends up in landfill sites in low-income communities. Plastic waste pollution exacerbates existing hygiene and sanitation challenges. Improper waste management is responsible for 60 per cent of malaria, diarrhea and pneumonia cases in children — diseases **(26)** _____ _____in Côte d'Ivoire.

Once it is fully operational, the factory will recycle 9,600 tonnes of plastic waste a year and provide **(27)** _____ in a formalized recycling market. Nine classrooms have been built in Gonzagueville, Divo and Toumodi using plastic bricks made in Colombia, demonstrating the viability of the construction methods and materials.

"We partnered with UNICEF on this **(28)** _____ _____ a social impact. By turning plastic pollution into an opportunity, we want to help lift women out of poverty and leave a better world for children," said Isabel Cristina Gamez, Co-Founder and CEO, Conceptos Plasticos.

67

The bricks will be made from 100 per cent plastic and are fire resistant. They are 40 per cent cheaper, 20 per cent lighter **(29)** _____ _____ building materials. They are also waterproof, well insulated and designed to resist heavy wind.

Alongside investment to build in Côte d'Ivoire, plans are also under **(30)** _____ _____ the region, and potentially beyond. West and central Africa accounts for one-third of the world's primary school age children and one-fifth of lower secondary age children who are out of school.

"Sometimes, embedded deep within our most pressing challenges are promising opportunities," said Fore. "This project is more than just a waste management and education infrastructure project; it is a functioning metaphor—the growing challenge of plastic waste turned into literal building blocks for a future generation of children."

21.   A.   a broken factory it had on first-of-its-kind ground to
         B.   it had broken ground on a first-of-its-kind factory to
         C.   to a first-of-its-kind factory on broken ground it had
         D.   it had to broken on a first-of-its-kind ground factory

22.   A.   that solutions for of the challenges major education some
         B.   solutions for some of the major education challenges that
         C.   of education for some the major challenges that solutions
         D.   the that of for solutions major some challenges education

23.   A.   children in Côte d'Ivoire, reduced classrooms plastic waste for
         B.   classrooms for children in Côte d'Ivoire, reduced plastic waste
         C.   plastic for children in classrooms, waste Côte d'Ivoire reduced
         D.   waste in Côte d'Ivoire classrooms, for reduced plastic children

24.   A.   collected plastic from in recycled polluted areas and around
         B.   plastic recycled and polluted areas from collected around in
         C.   polluted plastic collected from around recycled areas in and
         D.   recycled plastic collected from polluted areas in and around

25.   A.   championed has the inception project its from
         B.   from championed has its inception the project
         C.   has championed the project from its inception
         D.   its the championed project from inception has

26.
   A. among that are children of the leading causes death for
   B. causes death leading of among for the children are that
   C. for children that death are among the leading causes of
   D. that are among the leading causes of death for children

27.
   A. a source of income to women living in poverty
   B. income to women of a source in poverty living
   C. living women a source to poverty in income of
   D. poverty to women living in a source of income

28.
   A. because we want our project to have business model
   B. business model to have our project we want because
   C. project because we want our business model to have
   D. to have our business project model because we want

29.
   A. and will last hundreds of years longer than conventional
   B. conventional of years and will last hundreds longer than
   C. of years than conventional and hundreds will last longer
   D. than hundreds of years and will last longer conventional

30.
   A. other countries in way to scale this project to
   B. scale to project to other countries in way this
   C. countries in way to scale this project to other
   D. way to scale this project to other countries in

IV. Choose from among the four alternatives the one that best completes the following sentence.

31. An uneasy calm _____ in Indian-administered Kashmir on Monday as people celebrated a major Islamic festival during a severe crackdown after India moved to strip the disputed region of its constitutional _____ and imposed an indefinite curfew.

    A. ceased – disruption   B. prevailed – autonomy

    C. erupted – hiatus   D. waned – reform

32. Officials from China's northwestern Xinjiang region said Tuesday that most of the people detained in the area's _____ re-education centers have been moved out of the facilities and have signed "work contracts" with local companies, but those _____ have been challenged by accounts from Uighurs and Kazakhs who say their relatives remain missing.

    A. contentious – assertions   B. righteous – petitions

    C. vehement – arrests   D. promising – accusations

33. Tens of thousands of Russians _____ what a monitoring group called the country's biggest political protest for eight years on Saturday, _____ a crackdown to demand free elections to Moscow's city legislature.

    A. organized – launching   B. dismissed – tightening

    C. staged – defying   D. filed – infringing

34. Ten years after the start of a violent _____ in north-east Nigeria plunged the country into a humanitarian crisis that is "still far from over", the United Nations and its aid partners have _____ the need to "collectively redouble efforts" to help the most vulnerable.

    A. storm – underestimated   B. uprising – served

    C. insurgency – underscored   D. hatred – marginalized

35. For weeks, representatives of Venezuelan President Nicolas Maduro and his _____ successor, opposition leader Juan Guaido, have been shuttling back and forth to Barbados trying to agree on a common path out of the country's prolonged political _____.

    A. legitimate – impasse   B. would-be – standoff

    C. interim – detention   D. prospective – outcome

36. Deeply concerned about the new rule _____ from asylum the majority of people crossing the southern land border of the United States, the UN refugee agency, UNHCR, has warned that the 'severe' measure will endanger vulnerable people _____ international protection from violence or persecution.

A. granting − in light of
B. stipulating − with regard to
C. requiring − on behalf of
D. barring − in need of

37. Japan on Monday urged Iran to follow its commitments _____ a 2015 nuclear agreement with major powers and refrain from taking further actions to undermine it, after Tehran said it had started enriching uranium _____ the limit set by the deal.

A. under − above
B. toward − within
C. against − below
D. to − at

38. An independent review into how the UN System operated in Myanmar in the years leading up to the mass _____ of the Rohingya following serious human rights abuses, has concluded there were "systemic and structural failures" that prevented a unified strategy from being _____.

A. influx − endangered
B. murder − applied
C. excess − shrouded
D. exodus − implemented

39. North Korea fired two "new-type" projectiles from its east coast, the South Korean military said Friday — the country's third launch in just over a week, but one that U.S. President Donald Trump looked to _____ — as a trade and history clash between Tokyo and Seoul threatened joint efforts to _____ Pyongyang's nuclear program.

A. grapple with − retaliate against
B. play down − rein in
C. search for − rule out
D. reel from − give up

40. Protecting a potentially vulnerable _____ versus the public's need to know: A U.S. newspaper's publication of information on the man whose complaint led to an _____ inquiry into U.S. President Donald Trump has sparked controversy and debate.

A. informant − arraignment
B. accuser − exoneration
C. whistleblower − impeachment
D. suspect − indictment

71

V. Choose from among the underlined phrases the one that is grammatically or idiomatically incorrect.

41. (**A**) Just seven months after their last meeting in Argentina, (**B**) leaders of the Group of 20 nations gather in Osaka (**C**) this week to once again take up issues ranging from global trade (**D**) and dealing with maritime plastic waste.

42. (**A**) Two-third of the largely medieval roof of Notre Dame cathedral in Paris (**B**) have "gone" after the devastating fire in Paris on Monday evening, (**C**) but UN cultural experts are standing by to offer (**D**) help where it is needed in rebuilding the iconic structure.

43. (**A**) Tens of thousands rallied in a large Hong Kong (**B**) suburb on Sunday, driving by abiding anger at the government's handling (**C**) of an extradition bill that has revived fears of China (**D**) tightening its grip over the ex-British colony and dismantling its freedoms.

44. A marked escalation (**A**) in fighting has put tens of thousands of children (**B**) in northwest Syria at "imminent risk of injury, death (**C**) and displaced", the United Nations Children's Fund's (UNICEF) (**D**) chief warned on Thursday.

45. (**A**) An updated assessment by a United Nations Environment (**B**) Programme-administered treaty has (**C**) confirmed that poaching continues to threaten (**D**) the long-term survive of the African elephant.

46. The government (**A**) announced Monday it is tightened (**B**) regulations on the export of several chemicals (**C**) used in chip and smartphone production (**D**) to South Korea amid the row with Seoul over wartime forced labor.

47. (**A**) Stocks sank deeper across the board (**B**) on the Tokyo Stock Exchange Wednesday, (**C**) as heightened trade tensions between the United States and China (**D**) will continue to chill investor sentiment.

48. Russian President Vladimir Putin (**A**) has suggested that his country have (**B**) no plan to hand over four (**C**) Russian-held northwestern Pacific islands to Japan, (**D**) according to a Russian national television program aired Saturday.

49. (A) <u>Without increased support, the</u> health, education (B) <u>and well-being of at least</u> 327,000 children (C) <u>from Venezuela are living as migrants and</u> (D) <u>refugees in Colombia will be in jeopardy</u>, the UN Children's Fund (UNICEF) warned on Monday.

50. The UN Children's Fund (UNICEF) said (A) <u>on Monday that much great protection</u> (B) <u>for educational facilities was</u> (C) <u>needed across Afghanistan where</u> attacks (D) <u>against schools have increased three-fold</u> in just one year.

73

Choose from among the four alternatives the one that most closely corresponds to the meaning of words in bold type and blanks in the following passage.

What are the main obstacles to international cooperation among states? For some scholars, the obstacles are **(51) traced to** the concern by national policymakers that even if all states gain from cooperation (an increase in absolute gains), some will do so more than others thereby enhancing their power. In short, states are primarily concerned with the distribution of gains from cooperation (or relative gains). For other scholars, such concerns are less important than the possibility that particular states will **(52) defect from** cooperative arrangements to enhance their own interests, regardless of the distribution of gains from international cooperation.

In international relations theory, the debate is usually framed as taking place between neorealists and neoliberal institutionalists. Neorealism and neoliberal institutionalism are the dominant theories of international relations **(53)** _____ mainstream North American international relations scholarship. Much of the debate in the field has been articulated in terms of disagreements between these two approaches. However, these two theories actually share many fundamental assumptions. Neorealism is the more dominant theory. It argues that states act in accordance with the material structural incentives of the international system. State behaviour reflects the position of states within the international system. States' interests and strategies are based on calculations about their positions in the system. **(54)** _____, states seek to, at least, maintain their relative positions in the system. The greater a state's capabilities, the higher it is in the international hierarchy of power, and the greater its influence on the international stage. The structure of the international system is defined by this distribution of capabilities among states. The neorealist understanding of state behaviour is underpinned by five core assumptions:

1. The first and most fundamental is the assumption of anarchy, a lack of **(55) overarching** authority within the international system. This means that there is no power beyond states themselves that can enforce international agreements or protect the legitimate interests of states.
2. States possess military power and can be dangerous to each other. To some neorealists, power is reducible to military capabilities.
3. States can never be certain of the intentions of other states. An ally one day may be an enemy the next.
4. States are motivated by a concern with survival.
5. States are **(56) quintessentially** rational actors.

Anarchy means that states must always be preoccupied with issues of security and their survival; they can rely only on themselves, and fear other states. If states do not act in accordance with the demands of anarchy, they will be weaker as a result. Using this logic, neorealists depict international cooperation as extremely difficult to achieve. States will avoid cooperation if other states benefit relatively more from a cooperative relationship.

Neoliberal institutionalism attempts to use the spare, self-interested rational actor assumptions of neorealism to show that cooperation under anarchy is possible within the international system. Neoliberals attribute this cooperation to the ability of international institutions and regimes to **(57)** _____ the effects of anarchy. Neoliberal institutionalists describe states as being rational egoists – they are narrowly self-interested and concerned only with increasing their own utility. When calculating their own utility, they have little interest in the utility functions of other states. As such, if a cooperative endeavour is mutually beneficial, states may engage in that cooperative behaviour.

Finally, it should be noted that neoliberals generally restrict their theory to economic interactions, believing the dynamics of cooperation to be much more difficult to achieve in security affairs. Most neoliberals accept the neorealist **(58)** _____ an anarchic international system. Again, anarchy indicates a lack of overarching authority which means a lack of enforcement mechanisms to ensure state compliance with international agreements. As a result, neoliberalism identifies a fear of cheating and defection as the major **(59) impediments** to cooperation between states. This fear prevents cooperation even when it is rational for states to work together to their mutual benefit.

Institutions or regimes address this fear in three distinct ways: First, they create a sense of legal liability (i.e. a sense of obligation between states to adhere to rules and agreements). Second, they reduce transaction costs between states (the cost of interactions both within and between issue areas, and the cost of rules being broken). Finally, they provide transparency and information about issueareas and state actions. This is the most important function of regimes. The overall effect of regimes is to reduce uncertainty within the system, **(60)** _____ allowing states to cooperate more fully. Therefore, regimes mitigate the effects of anarchy. Neorealism and neoliberalism both study regimes as the instruments of states. The effectiveness of a regime is directly measured by the level of compliance with its rules by states.

51. In this context, "traced to" is best replaced by
    A.   acquired with   B.   blocked by
    C.   emergent from   D.   reliant on

52. In this context, "defect from" is closest in meaning to
    A.   abandon   B.   blunder
    C.   distrust   D.   mistake

53. **From the context, the underlined blank could best be filled with**
    A. around   B. as well as
    C. withholding   D. within

54. **From the context, the underlined blank could best be filled with**
    A. However,   B. In contrast,
    C. Thus,   D. Whilst

55. **In this context, "overarching" is closest in meaning to**
    A. dwarfing   B. genuine
    C. supreme   D. worthwhile

56. **In this context, "quintessentially" is closest in meaning to**
    A. blatantly   B. defiantly
    C. deliberately   D. typically

57. **From the context, the underlined blank could best be filled with**
    A. emulate   B. instigate
    C. mitigate   D. propagate

58. **From the context, the underlined blank could best be filled with**
    A. characterization of   B. clash over
    C. contention with   D. criticism against

59. **In this context, "impediments" is best replaced by**
    A. complications   B. impairments
    C. obstacles   D. snags

60. **From the context, the underlined blank could best be filled with**
    A. conversely   B. nevertheless
    C. owing to   D. thereby

Ⅶ. Choose from among the four alternatives the one that best explains each of the underlined words or phrases in the context of the article below.

More than 500 million people today live in areas affected by erosion linked to climate change, the UN warned on Thursday, before urging all countries to (61) **commit to** sustainable land use to help limit greenhouse gas emissions before it is too late. Speaking at the launch of a Special Report on Climate Change and Land by the UN Intergovernmental Panel on Climate Change (IPCC) in Geneva, experts highlighted how the rise in global temperatures, linked to increasing pressures on fertile soil, risked (62) **jeopardizing** food security for the planet.

Humans affect more than 70 per cent of ice-free land and a quarter is already degraded, noted Valérie Masson-Delmotte, Co-Chair of one of three Working Groups that contributed to the (63) **bumper** 1,200-page report. "Today 500 million people live in areas that experience desertification," she told journalists. "People living in already degraded or desertified areas are increasingly negatively affected by climate change." This soil degradation has a direct impact on the amount of carbon the earth is able to contain, Dr. Masson-Delmotte explained.

Amid recent reports that more an 820 million people are undernourished around the world, Co-Chair of another Working Group, Jim Skea, highlighted the fact that up to 30 per cent of food is lost or wasted. In future, countries should consider all options to tackle loss and waste, thereby reducing the pressure on land and the resulting greenhouse gas emissions, including by growing plant-based, or so-called "bio" fuels, he said.

"Limiting global warming to 1.5 or even two degrees (Celsius) will involve removing carbon dioxide from the atmosphere and land has a critical role to play in carbon dioxide removal," Dr. Skea (64) **insisted**. "Agricultural practices can help build up carbon in soils, but it could also mean using more bio-energy with or without carbon capture and storage and expanding forests."

Produced by 107 scientists from more than 50 countries across all regions of the world—with more than half of the contributing authors from developing nations—the IPCC report provides a peer-based (65) **review** of the latest research on land use today. According to the IPCC report, agriculture, forestry and other land use contribute to around a quarter of greenhouse gas emissions, a fact that policy-makers should consider when considering how they should invest to adapt to and (66) **mitigate** the effects of climate change.

"Reducing greenhouse gas emissions from all sectors is essential if we want to keep temperatures rises below two degrees Celsius," said Debra Roberts, Co-Chair of Working Group II, before (67) **cautioning** that there were "limits to the scale of energy crops and afforestation that could be used to achieve this goal".

The need for immediate action in the (68) **face** of a warming planet was underlined by another Working Group Co-Chair, Hans-Otto Pörtner, who stressed that there was "no possibility for anybody to say, 'Oh, climate change is happening and we (will) just adapt to it.' The capacity to adapt is (**69**) <u>limited</u>." Despite the challenges many countries face from climate-change related pressures on land, positive action was needed now, Dr Pörtner maintained, amid estimates that the global population is set to reach around 10 billion by 2050.

"There are some regions and some places, especially in the lower latitudes where vulnerability is extreme," he said. "But even in those countries, when there is an emphasis on adaptation in their development strategies, mitigation should play a key role."

Before Thursday's report launch, the text had to be assessed and approved by 195 Member States, a process that took longer than expected on Wednesday. In addition to the Special Report on Climate Change and Land, the IPCC plans to release its latest findings on the Ocean and Cryosphere in a Changing Climate next month, ahead of the UN Climate Action Summit on 23 September in New York.

The IPCC was established by the United Nations Environment Programme (UN Environment) and the World Meteorological Organization (WMO) in 1988 to provide policymakers with regular scientific (**70**) <u>assessments</u> concerning climate change, its implications and potential future risks, and to put forward adaptation and mitigation strategies.

61.   <u>commit to</u>

     A.   agree to ban   B.   endeavor to terminate
     C.   pledge to practice   D.   seek to eradicate

62.   <u>jeopardizing</u>

     A.   imitating   B.   inoculating
     C.   imperiling   D.   impersonating

63.   <u>bumper</u>

     A.   derisory   B.   mammoth
     C.   meager   D.   paltry

64.   <u>insisted</u>

     A.   denied   B.   forbade
     C.   maintained   D.   negated

65.   <u>review</u>

     A.   apparel   B.   appraisal
     C.   penalty   D.   triviality

66. **mitigate**
  A. abate
  B. aggravate
  C. exacerbate
  D. rebate

67. **cautioning**
  A. disallowing
  B. forswearing
  C. presaging
  D. refuting

68. **face**
  A. euphoria
  B. expectation
  C. improbability
  D. unlikelihood

69. **limited**
  A. confidential
  B. privileged
  C. restricted
  D. top-secret

70. **assessments**
  A. conjectures
  B. hearsays
  C. taxations
  D. judgments

VIII. Fill in each of the following blanks with the most appropriate of the four alternatives as required by the context.

News of the nuclear explosion at a military base in the far north of Russia trickled out slowly.

First came the bulletins on state media of at least two people killed in a mysterious accident. Then came news of a **(71)** _____ in radiation in the area, and footage reportedly showing doctors in hazmat suits treating the victims. Finally, on Aug. 13 – five days after the blast – the Kremlin appeared to come clean, confirming that five nuclear scientists and at least two others had died while testing one of the newest weapons in President Vladimir Putin's arsenal.

"Accidents, unfortunately, happen," Putin's spokesman told reporters on a conference call that morning.

(72) _____, for nuclear experts and negotiators, there was a sense that this particular accident had been waiting to happen. Putin had promised the world a new type of nuclear missile during his state of the nation address last year, a **(73)** _____ he illustrated with an animation of a rocket landing with a bang in Florida. But the types of weapons he was bragging about—from nuclear-armed cruise missiles to underwater drones packed with radioactive materials—are notoriously difficult and dangerous to build.

"The systems that Putin has been talking about publicly are rather exotic and not as far along, or anywhere close to being ready for **(74)** _____," says Lynn Rusten, a nuclear expert who oversaw arms control issues at the National Security Council under the Obama Administration. "That is why the U.S. hasn't pursued them."

At least not yet. But one lesson from last week's explosion may be that any country, be it Russia, the U.S. or China, can pursue such weapons without violating any rules. That's because, over the past few years, the system of treaties that supports the world's security architecture has been **(75)** _____ along with the diplomatic ties between Russia and the West.

On August 2, after accusing Russia of deploying banned weapons for years, the U.S. formally withdrew from the Intermediate-Range Nuclear Forces (INF) treaty, which was signed in 1987 to contain both countries' arsenals. An even more ambitious nuclear disarmament deal between the U.S. and Russia, known as New START, is due to expire in 2021, and there isn't much hope of it being renewed. Putin said in June that he would be willing to extend the treaty for another five years. But John Bolton, the National Security Adviser to President Trump, has said the U.S. is "unlikely" to go along.

The result is a world with less constraints on nuclear weapons, and more countries with the ability to build them. "There's a qualitative arms race going on," says Gary Samore, who helped negotiate New START. "There's a whole new class of strategic weapons that the U.S., Russia and China are working on that are not **(76)** _____ to any arms control treaties," Samore tells TIME.

80

2019年
第2回
問題

The explosion on Aug. 8 highlights the danger of that new reality. State news agency Itar-Tass reported that the blast was powerful enough to throw several staff members from Rosatom, the Russian state nuclear agency, off the testing platform and into the White Sea. (**77**) _____ no jump in radiation levels has yet been detected outside Russia, officials across northern Europe have expressed concern that the damaged weapon could contaminate the sea and pose a danger to their citizens. The Russian village closest to the blast site was reportedly ordered to evacuate on Monday, but local officials said the next day that no evacuation would take place.

The secrecy around the explosion highlights another unpleasant fact about the nuclear era: Governments hate to admit their mistakes when it comes to handling their most dangerous technology, and the desire to hide those mistakes has often made them even deadlier.

After the explosion at the Chernobyl nuclear power plant in 1986, the Soviet authorities waited days before evacuating the area, (**78**) _____ many thousands of its citizens to extreme levels of radiation. During the first year of Putin's presidency in 2000, a Russian submarine known as the Kursk sank in the Barents Sea, and his generals were so obsessed with protecting the vessel's nuclear secrets that they refused foreign help with the rescue effort for several days. By the time Norwegian divers were allowed to reach the submarine, all 118 sailors on board were dead.

Russia's citizens, like the rest of the world, do not yet know the full extent of the damage caused by last week's explosion near the city of Severodvinsk. Learning that will take time and a level of (**79**) _____ that the Kremlin has not yet been able to meet.

But even the available details are enough to understand that this was not simply a case of rotten luck. (**80**) _____ the rate at which the present arms race is accelerating, and the legal constraints on building these kind of weapons are unraveling, such events seem all but inevitable.

"We're entering a period of intense competition," says Michael Carpenter, who formerly served as the top Russia expert at the Pentagon. "How we manage it is vitally important to our national security." And, when it comes to managing nuclear weapons, to the security of the world.

71.   A.   spike   B.   decree
       C.   fallout   D.   deterioration

72.   A.   Therefore   B.   Moreover
       C.   Instead   D.   Indeed

73.   A.   pledge   B.   skirmish
       C.   screed   D.   perk

74.   A.   disposition   B.   deployment
        C.   dispute   D.   requisition

75.   A.   protracted   B.   functioning
        C.   unraveling   D.   sanctioned

76.   A.   due   B.   subject
        C.   included   D.   ratified

77.   A.   Though   B.   Because
        C.   After   D.   When

78.   A.   jeopardizing   B.   causing
        C.   exposing   D.   depriving

79.   A.   contamination   B.   scrutiny
        C.   emancipation   D.   transparency

80.   A.   Given   B.   Regardless of
        C.   Despite   D.   Below

IX.   **Write a short essay in English of 150-200 words as your answer to the following question:**

Why is gender equality a core goal for the UN to advance in the world?

マークシート記入例

東京の本会場で<u>A級</u>を受験する、<u>国連 太郎</u>さん、受験番号が「<u>東京01-20001</u>」、生年月日が「<u>1980年10月24日</u>」の場合の記入例です。

【受験番号/氏名】
それぞれ受験票の記載通りに記入してください。

受験番号	東京01-20001
氏 名	国連 太郎

【受験地区】
受験記号・番号の、都道府県部分を塗りつぶしてください。

【会場番号】
都道府県部分に続く2桁の数字を塗りつぶしてください。

【受験番号】
ハイフン（−）以降の5桁の数字を塗りつぶしてください。

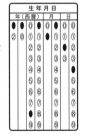

【受験級】
「A」と記入し、下段のA級部分を塗りつぶしてください。

【生年月日】
4桁の西暦・月・日を塗りつぶしてください。
10未満の月・日の十の位は、「0」を塗りつぶしてください。

※HB以上の鉛筆を用いてマークをしてください。

※他の地区から会場を変更して受験する場合でも、受験票に記載されている受験地区・会場番号をマークしてください。

83

2019年
第2回試験

解答・解説

　　　　　　　　　　　　　　　　　　　　＊〔　〕内は訳出上の補足や説明

> **I** 『新 わかりやすい国連の活動と世界』に基づき，
> 空所を埋めるのに最も適切なものを 4 つの選択肢の中から 1 つ選びなさい。

1.　解答：C

訳例　総会の定例会議は毎年 9 月の第 3 火曜日に始まり，12 月半ばまで続く。定例
　　　会議は，場合によって翌年に再開されることもある（『新 わかりやすい国連の
　　　活動と世界』p.54。以下，書名略）。

2.　解答：A

訳例　総会の権限のもとで機能する経済社会理事会（ECOSOC）は，国連およびその
　　　専門機関の経済社会活動を調整するための機関である（同 p.56）。

3.　解答：D

訳例　安全保障理事国は，それぞれ 1 票の投票権を持つ。手続き事項の決定には，15
　　　理事国のうち少なくとも 9 理事国の賛成を必要とする（同 p.55）。

4.　解答：B

訳例　1982 年の国連海洋法条約は，国連の最も目覚ましい業績の 1 つとして一般に
　　　高く評価されている。この条約は，航海，漁業，鉱物資源開発や科学的探査な
　　　ど，実質的に海洋利用のすべての側面に適用される包括的な規則を定めている
　　　（同 p.149）。

5.　解答：A

訳例　国連の通常予算は 2 年ごとに総会によって承認される（同 p.62）。

6.　解答：D

訳例　UNHCR の基本的な職務は，定義によれば母国の保護を受けていない難民に国
　　　際的保護を与えることである（同 p.143）。

7.　解答：D

訳例　国際司法裁判所は，総会および安全保障理事会が個々に行う投票によって選出された 15 人の裁判官によって構成される。裁判官は，国籍によってではなく個々の資格によって選出される……（同 p.60）。

8.　解答：C

訳例　「国際連合」という名称は，フランクリン・D・ルーズベルト米大統領の発案による。正式に採用されたのは 1942 年，26 カ国の代表が「ヒットラー主義打倒の闘い」において協力を誓い，連合国宣言に署名した時点であった（同 p.43）。

9.　解答：C

訳例　発足時の加盟国 51 カ国は，サンフランシスコ会議に出席したか，それ以前に連合国宣言に署名し，のち国連憲章に調印，これを批准した国々である（同 p.45）。

10.　解答：D

訳例　総会は，この宣言を「すべての国民と国家が達成すべき共通の基準」と呼んだ（同 p.143）。

II　下線を引いた動詞の最も適切な変化形を 4 つの選択肢の中から 1 つ選びなさい。

11.　解答：B

解説　下線の compete から to succeed her までを下線前の the two men を修飾する形容詞句とする。文脈から争いは現在進んでいる意味になるので，D. to compete は不適。

12.　解答：D

解説　主語はセンテンス頭の May〔英首相〕。起きた事態（米大統領の暴言）に対する同首相の現時点での考え方を示す文であるので，現在形がよい。

13.　解答：A

解説　文脈より the two politicians がメイ首相の後継となるのはこれより後の予定であるから，その意味を表す to 不定詞で the two politicians を後置修飾する形が適切。

87

14. 解答：B

解説 下線部は if 節の主語 anyone の述語動詞であるが，その仮定の意味内容は単純で C の完了的な意味は適さない。B. said（仮定法過去）とすることで現実に起きにくいと考えられる仮定を提示している。

15. 解答：B

解説 文脈から ask は受け身とすべきであることが分かる。主語はセンテンス頭の Hunt で，when [he was] asked のように主語と be 動詞が省略されている。

16. 解答：B

解説 センテンス頭の It が仮主語，意味上の主語は下線部以下となるので，下線部動詞を to 不定詞とする。

17. 解答：A

解説 下線部前の was asked の時点でトランプ発言が現在のものとして受け取られていると考えられるので，時制の一致により過去形を取る。

18. 解答：D

解説 動詞 rattle はここでは他動詞で「混乱させる」の意。文脈から受け身となるが，時の副詞句 in the last two weeks に合う現在完了形とする。

19. 解答：A

解説 センテンス頭の responded by に続く calling と下線部動詞が意味的に並立するので，動名詞を置くのが正しい。

20. 解答：C

解説 下線部前の talking to が付帯状況を表す分詞構文で，分詞としてもう1つ claiming が添えられている構造をつかむ。下線部動詞は talking to に続く分詞句内にあるため定動詞は不適。

訳例 テリーザ・メイ英首相と，同首相の後継者を争う男性〔候補〕2人は，ドナルド・トランプ米大統領が有色人種の女性議員4人を攻撃したことを非難した

が，月曜日には大統領発言を人種差別的と呼ぶことを控える〔姿勢に転じた〕。

トランプ氏は日曜日，この〔4人の〕リベラルな民主党員について，「壊れて犯罪まみれの」出身国へ帰ったらどうか〔など〕とツイッターに投稿していた。4人はいずれも米国市民で，うち3人は米国生まれ。

英EU離脱をめぐり辞意を表明し，来週退陣となるメイ〔首相〕は，「女性らを取り上げた言葉づかいはまったく認められるものではない」との考えだ。ジェームズ・スラック〔首相〕報道官が明らかにした。

メイ氏に代わる保守党党首兼英首相を選ぶ決選投票に残ったボリス・ジョンソン氏とジェレミー・ハント外相の政治家も同調した。

ジョンソン氏はトランプ氏発言について，「現代の多民族国家では到底認められない」と述べた。

同氏はハント氏との討論会の中で，「偉大な多民族・多文化社会の指導者ならば，人を出身地へと送り返すことについてあのような言葉づかいをすることは断じて許されない」とした。

政治的に対立する〔ハント氏〕も同じ思いを口にした。

同氏は中国人の妻を持つ。「私には中国人とのハーフの子供が3人いる。その子たちに『中国に帰れ』と言う人がいたら，まったくゾッとするだろう」と語った。

ただ，外相としてイギリス外交を率いる〔立場から〕，トランプ氏の発言を人種差別的と思うかとの問いには言葉を濁し，米国は英国の最も近い同盟国だとした上で，次のように述べた。

「米国の大統領についてそうした言葉を使うことは事態の改善にはつながらない」。

同じくジョンソン氏も，トランプ氏の発言が人種差別的かと聞かれ，答えを拒んだ。

これらの発言は，〔大西洋を挟む〕英米関係にとってピリピリした〔最近の〕時期に重なっている。両国の関係はこの2週間，在米英国大使が打ったトランプ政権を批判する外交公電が漏洩し，メール・オン・サンデー紙がこれを公開したことで混乱を極めている。

トランプ氏はこれに対しツイッターで，キム・ダロック〔英〕大使を「非常に愚かだ」と〔罵倒〕し，冷たくあしらった。ダロック氏は「これ以上職務を遂行できない」として辞任した。

トランプ氏は女性議員に対する発言を自ら擁護し，月曜日には再びツイッター上で民主党議員4人の謝罪を要求するとともに，「この人たち，そして&そのひどい&むかつくような言動に大勢の人が怒っている」と主張した。

空所を埋めるのに文法的・論理的に最もふさわしいものを
4つの選択肢の中から1つ選びなさい。

21. 解答：B

解説 空所前の announced on Monday that に注目して that 節を形成する B を選び，空所後の convert ... にもうまくつながることを確認する。

22. 解答：B

解説 空所冒頭は文脈から名詞（句）が入ると予測し，空所末は後の Africa's children and communities face が関係節になる可能性を考慮すると，B が適切。末尾に関係代名詞 that が置かれており，うまくつながる。

23. 解答：B

解説 空所前が ... is threefold となっているので，空所冒頭から3つの名詞句の並列を予想し，空所後の and 以下がその3番目だろうと目を付ける。また，2つ目の名詞句の最後が in the environment につながることにも注意。

24. 解答：D

解説 特に前置詞の用法から文法的に正しいものはDのみ。

25. 解答：C

解説 空所前の who が Dr. Aboubacar Kampo を先行詞とする主格関係代名詞であることを見抜いて正しい関係節となるものを選ぶ。

26. 解答：D

解説 空所前の diseases は上の行の malaria, diarrhea, and pneumonia cases ... と同格に置かれており，そのあとにこの diseases を修飾する形容詞句が続くことを予測する。

27. 解答：A

解説 空所前の動詞 provide に着目して「～に～を供給する」の意味を予測し，文法的に正しいものを選ぶ。

28. 解答：C

解説 文法的には D も可能だが to have out business project model の部分の意味が通らない。

29. 解答：A

解説 空所前に 40 per cent cheaper, 20 per cent lighter とあることから，空所は and に続いて 3 番目の比較表現となっていることが予測できる。

30. 解答：D

解説 空所前の plans are also under に続くものとして under way という成句が予測できるので，D で前後の意味が整合することを確認すればよい。

訳例 国連児童基金（ユニセフ）とコロンビアの社会的企業が月曜日，革新的な提携を結び，「西アフリカのコートジボワールで回収されたプラスチック廃棄物からプラスチック製のモジュールレンガを生産する世界初の工場の建設に着手した」と発表した。組み立てが簡単で，耐久性があり，低価格のこのレンガは，コートジボワールで多数必要とされている教室建物の建築に利用される。

ユニセフのヘンリエッタ・フォア事務局長は次のように話している。「この工場は，アフリカの子供たちやコミュニティーが抱えている教育面でのいくつかの大きな課題に対して，高度で，しかも拡張適用できる解決策をもたらす最先端の工場となる。可能性としては，コートジボワールの子供を教える教室を増やす，環境中のプラスチック廃棄物を削減する，最も弱い立場にある家庭の収入源を増やす，という 3 つの点が挙げられる」。

コートジボワールでは，学び場がない子供たちのニーズに対応するため，教室 15,000 室が必要とされている。この教室不足を解消するため，ユニセフでは，コンセプトス・プラスティコス社と提携し，〔コートジボワール最大の都市〕アビジャンとその周辺の汚染地区から回収してリサイクルしたプラスチックを利用して，最も緊急に教室を必要としている子供 2 万 5,000 人以上が学べる教室 500 室を今後 2 年で設けることにした。将来的には建築件数を増やすことも可能だ。

〔現地〕ユニセフ代表で，この事業を当初から支持してきたアブバカル・カンポ博士〔医師・公衆衛生専門家〕は次のように話している。「コートジボワールの学校の子供たちが抱える大きな問題の 1 つに，教室不足がある。教室がないか，あっても過密状態であり，学習しにくく，不快な環境となっている。一部の地域では，貧しい地区の幼稚園児が初めて，他の 100 人足らずの子供たちといっしょに授業を受けられるようになった。学校に自分たちの居場所が

あるとこれまで決して思わなかった子供たちが，新しいピカピカの教室で勉強し，力をつけることができるようになる」。

　プラスチック廃棄物の発生量は，アビジャンだけでも1日当たり280トン以上にのぼる。そのうちリサイクルに回るのは約5％と少なく，残りのほとんどは低所得者が住む地域にある埋め立て地に廃棄される。プラスチック廃棄物による汚染は，これまでもあった衛生面の問題をさらに悪化させる。子供のマラリア，下痢，肺炎は，不適切な廃棄物管理を原因とするものが60％にのぼっている。これらは，コートジボワールの子供の死因の最上位を占める病気である。

　工場はフル稼働すると年間9,600トンのプラスチック廃棄物をリサイクルし，正式なリサイクル市場を〔形成することで〕貧困生活を送る女性たちの収入源となる。ゴンザゲビル，ディーボ，トゥモディでは，コロンビア産のプラスチックレンガを使って教室9室がすでに完成しており，建築方法と建築材料の実用性が実証された。

　コンセプトス・プラスティコス社の共同設立者でCEOを務めるイサベル・クリスティーナ・ガメス氏は次のように話している。「当社がこの事業でユニセフと提携したのは，当社のビジネスモデルが社会的な影響を及ぼすようになってほしいと考えたからだ。プラスチック汚染を転じてチャンスにすることで，当社は女性を貧困から救い出し，子供たちのためにより良い世界を残したい」。

　レンガは100％プラスチックで作られ，耐火性を備えている。従来の建築材料に比べて40％価格が安く，20％軽量で，何百年も長持ちする。また，防水性，断熱性に優れ，強風にも耐えられるように設計されている。

　コートジボワールへの建築投資に加え，この事業をこの地域の他の国々へ拡大し，さらに他の地域へも拡大する可能性を秘めた計画が進められている。西アフリカおよび中央アフリカでは，小学校に通う年齢で学校に行っていない子供が世界全体の3分の1，前期中等学校〔中学校〕に当たる年齢の子供については世界全体の5分の1をそれぞれ占めている。

　フォア氏は次のように話している。「最も差し迫った難題の奥底には時として，有望な機会が隠されている。この事業は廃棄物管理と教育インフラの単なる事業ではない。悪化するプラスチック廃棄物問題を将来世代の子供たちのために文字どおり建築材料に転換するという，現実的に力を持つメタファーなのだ」。

IV 以下の文章に最も適切に当てはまる語句のペアを
4つの選択肢の中から1つ選びなさい。

31.　解答：B

解説　第1空所は1行目末以降 as people celebrated ... という文脈から B.

prevailed が選べる。第2空所も事実内容から B. autonomy が適切。

訳例 インドが〔実効〕支配するカシミールでは月曜日，不穏な静けさが広がっていた。インドがこの〔印パ間の〕紛争地域から憲法で認められた自治権を剥奪する挙を起こし，無期限の外出禁止令を発令した後の厳しい弾圧の下で〔この日〕，イスラム教の大きな祭り〔犠牲祭り〕が行われた。

---

32. 解答：A

解説 第1空所は，話題が新疆ウイグル自治区の再教育施設であることから，A. contentious がよい。第2空所は the people detained in the area's _____ re-education centers have been moved out the facilities and have signed "work contracts" with local companies という発言内容を指すので，A. assertions が選べる。

訳例 中国北西部，新疆〔ウイグル自治〕の当局者は火曜日，同地区に置かれ，論争の的となっている再教育センターに拘留された人々の大半が施設から移送され，現地企業との間で「労働契約」を交わしたと述べた。だが，こうした主張は，「親類が行方不明のままになっている」と〔訴える〕ウイグル人やカザフ人の話と食い違っている。

---

33. 解答：C

解説 第1空所は「人々が政治的抗議活動を行った」という文脈から A. organized と C. staged が残る。第2空所はその後の crackdown に注目して C. defying を選ぶ。

訳例 ロシアで土曜日，数万人がモスクワ市議会の自由選挙を求めて弾圧に抗し，〔大規模な〕政治的抗議行動を行った。ある監視団体によると過去8年間のロシアで最大のもの。

---

34. 解答：C

解説 第1空所は文脈から B. uprising と C. insurgency が残る。第2空所は，B. served だとすると，その現在完了形は現在までの継続の意味となり，センテンス頭の Ten years after ... と整合しない。

訳例 ナイジェリア北東部の暴力的な反乱が始まり，同国が人道危機に陥ってから10年〔となったが，〕危機は「依然として去っていない」。〔そうした中で〕国連とその連携先の援助団体が，最も弱い立場にある人々を助けるため「集団的取り組みを倍加する」必要性を強調した。

93

35. 解答：B

解説 第2空所はA. impasseかB. standoff，第1空所は事実関係からB. would-be を選ぶ。

訳例 ベネズエラのニコラス・マドゥロ大統領と，その後継を目指す野党指導者フアン・グアイド——その双方の代表者がこの数週間，長引く政治的な膠着状態を脱する共通の道筋について合意を結ぶべく，バルバドスとの間を行ったり来たりしている。

36. 解答：D

解説 第1空所は from asylum the majority of people の語順が通常とは反対になっており，from が「～に対して禁じる，阻む」の意味で使われる前置詞であることに着目し，D. barring を選ぶ。第2空所も前後関係から D. in need of がよい。

訳例 国連で難民問題を担当するUNHCRは，米国の南部陸上国境を越えて流入する大多数の人々の難民申請を妨げる新しいルールに対して大きな懸念を抱いており，暴力や迫害からの国際的な保護を必要とする弱い立場の人々がこの「厳しい」措置のために危険にさらされるとして警鐘を鳴らした。

37. 解答：A

解説 第1空所は前に follow its commitments とあることから，A. under が選べる。第2空所も A. above で事実関係に一致している。

訳例 日本はイランに対し月曜日，主要国との間で結んだ2015年核合意の下での確約を守り，この合意を損なう新たな行動を控えるよう求めた。イラン政府が，合意に定められた上限を超えるウラン濃縮を開始したと表明したことを受けたもの。

38. 解答：D

解説 第2空所は B. applied と D. implemented が残る。第1空所は mass ＿＿＿ of the Rohingya だけを考えれば B. murder も可能だが，次の following serious human rights abuses と意味的に重複する。ここで言われている事実内容からも D. exodus の方がよい。

訳例 ロヒンギャの人々が深刻な人権侵害の発生から集団脱出をするに至るまでの数年間に国連システムがミャンマーでどのように活動していたかを検討するため中立の立場から進められていた審査で，「組織的かつ構造的な失策」の結果，

統一的な戦略を実行できなかったとの結論が出された。

39.　解答：B

解説　第 1 空所は「発射は過去 1 週間余りで 3 回目となるが，大統領は _____ する考え」という文脈から，B. play down（重視しない）がよい。第 2 空所も文脈や事実関係から B. rein in が選べる。

訳例　日韓両政府間の貿易と歴史〔認識〕をめぐる衝突が，北朝鮮の核開発計画を抑え込む共同の取り組みに対する脅威となる中，韓国軍は金曜日，北朝鮮が東部海岸から 2 発の「新型」飛翔体を発射した，と発表した。発射は 1 週間余りで 3 回目となるが，ドナルド・トランプ米大統領は問題視しない考えだ。

40.　解答：C

解説　第 1 空所は直前直後だけでは絞りにくく，D. suspect のみ排除できる。第 2 空所の方で周知の事実関係から C. impeachment（弾劾）を選ぶ。

訳例　弱い立場となりうる内部告発者の保護か，国民が知る必要性か：ドナルド・トランプ米大統領の弾劾審査のきっかけとなった苦情を申し立てた男性に関する情報を米紙が公表したことから，〔さまざまな〕論議や論争が巻き起こった。

V

文法的，語法的にふさわしくないものを下線の中から 1 つ選びなさい。

41.　解答：D

解説　and dealing → to dealing。D の前の ranging に着目。ranging from ... to ... の形で頻繁に現れる。

訳例　G20 の首脳らは，前回のアルゼンチン会合から 7 カ月しか経たぬ今週，大阪に集まり，グローバル貿易や海洋プラスチックごみ対策などさまざまな問題についていま一度議論する。

42.　解答：A

解説　Two-third → two-thirds。

訳例　パリのノートル・ダム大聖堂は，月曜日夜に発生した大規模火災により，中世に造られた部分が大半を占める屋根のうち 3 分の 2 が「失われた」が，国連ユネスコの専門家らは，〔フランスを〕象徴するこの建造物の再建に必要な支援を提供しようといま準備を進めている。

43. 解答：B

解説 driving → driven。動詞 drive の意味上の主語と目的語は何かを考える。

訳例 かつてイギリスの植民地だった香港の大きな郊外地区で日曜日，数万人が集会を開いた。〔人々を動かしたのは〕中国が香港に対する支配を強め，自由を破壊するとの懸念を再燃させた逃亡犯条例〔改正〕案をめぐる〔香港特別行政区〕政府の対応に向けられた変わらぬ怒り〔である〕。

44. 解答：C

解説 displaced → displacement。前の imminent risk of に続いて並列する3つの名詞の3番目。

訳例 シリア北西部で子供たち数万人が戦闘の著しい激化によって「負傷や死，強制退去に遭う差し迫ったリスク」にさらされているとして，国連児童基金（ユニセフ）事務局長が木曜日，警鐘を鳴らした。

45. 解答：D

解説 survive → survival。前後 the long-term ... of から survive の名詞形とする。

訳例 国連環境計画が条約事務局となっている〔ワシントン〕条約に基づく最新の評価で，アフリカゾウが長期的に存続する上で密猟が引き続き脅威となっていることが確認された。

46. 解答：A

解説 tightened → tightening。動詞 tighten の主語 it は前の the government を指す。続く regulations が tighten の目的語。

訳例 徴用工をめぐる韓国政府との対立が続く中，政府は月曜日，〔半導体〕チップやスマートフォンの生産に使用される数種類の化学物質について，韓国への輸出規制を強化すると発表した。

47. 解答：D

解説 will continue → continued。主節の動詞 sank に時制を合わせる。

訳例 米中貿易摩擦の悪化で投資家心理が冷え込み続ける中，東京証券取引所の株価は水曜日，さらに全面安となった。

48. 解答：A

解説 have → has。前の動詞 suggested はこの場合「それとなく言う」の意なので，that 節内の動詞は仮定法現在（または should＋原形）ではなく，直接法となる。

訳例 土曜日に放送されたロシア国営テレビの番組によると，ロシアのウラジミル・プーチン大統領はロシアが占拠する北西太平洋四島について，日本に引き渡す計画がないことを示唆した。

49. 解答：C

解説 are living → living。センテンスの定動詞は 3 行目の will be。living ... は at least 327,000 children from Venezuela を修飾する現在分詞句。

訳例 国連児童基金（ユニセフ）は月曜日，コロンビアで移民や難民として暮らすベネズエラの子供たち 32 万 7,000 人以上について，支援の拡大がなければ健康・教育・幸福が危険にさらされると警鐘を鳴らした。

2019年
第2回
解答・解説

50. 解答：A

解説 great → greater。3 行目 where 以下の attacks ... have increased three-fold に着目して great を比較級とする。比較級を強める副詞 much にも留意。

訳例 国連児童基金（ユニセフ）は月曜日，アフガニスタンで学校に対する攻撃件数がわずか 1 年で 3 倍に増加しており，全土で教育施設に対してはるかに強力な保護が求められると述べた。

VI 以下の文章の中に含まれる太字の語句および空所の意味として文脈上最も近いものを 4 つの選択肢の中から 1 つ選びなさい。

51. 解答：C

解説 (traced ＞) trace to はこの場合「（原因を）さかのぼる，調べ出す」であるから，前置詞 to の後に the obstacles の原因が示されることになる。

52. 解答：A

解説 defect はこの場合，abandon a position or association, often in favor of an opposing one の意。

97

53. 解答：D

解説 空所前後は「～は北米の主流の国際関係論学界内において有力な国際関係の理論である」の意と推測される。

54. 解答：C

解説 空所前後は「各国家の利益と戦略は，このシステムにおける自国の地位に関する計算に基づく。_____，各国家はせめてこのシステムにおける自国の相対的な位置を維持しようとする」の意であるから，接続詞としては C.「それゆえ」が適切。

55. 解答：C

解説 overarching はこの場合 dominating or embracing all else の意であるから，最も近いのは C.「至高の」。

56. 解答：D

解説 quintessentially ＞ quintessential は, representing the perfect or most typical example of a quality の意。

57. 解答：C

解説 空所前後の意味は「新自由主義者は，このような協力は国際的な制度やレジームが持つ，無政府状態の影響を_____能力によって実現すると考える」。よって，C.「緩和する」が適切。

58. 解答：A

解説 空所前後の意味は「大半の新自由主義者は，『無政府状態の国際システム』という新現実主義による_____を受け入れている」であるから，下線部には A.「～という性格付け」が最適。

59. 解答：C

解説 impediments ＞ impediment は hindrance or interference の意。よって C.「障害物」がよい。

60.　解答：D

解説　空所前後の意味「レジームの全体的効果とは，システム内の不確実性を減少させることであり，＿＿＿＿＿ 各国家はより全面的に協力できるようになる」から考えて，空所には D.「それによって」が入る。

訳例　国家間の国際協力を阻む主な障害は何だろうか。一部の学者によれば，その障害の大元は国内政策立案者の次のような懸念にある。すなわち，すべての国家が協力によって利益を得るとしても（絶対的利益の増加），一部の国家が他の国家よりも多くの利益を得て力を強めることになるのではないか，という懸念である。つまり，国家は，協力から得られる利益の分配（または相対的利益）に第一義的な関心を持つのである。他の学者はそうした懸念よりも，国際協力から得られる利益の分配にかかわらず，特定の国家が自国の利益を高めるために協力体制を脱退する可能性の方を重要視する。

　　　国際関係論においては，以上の議論は通常，新現実主義者と新自由主義的制度主義者の間で行われている〔議論〕と考えられている。新現実主義と新自由主義的制度主義は，北米の主流の国際関係論学界内における有力な国際関係の理論である。この分野での議論の多くは，この２つのアプローチ間の不一致という形で行われてきた。しかし，両理論は実は基本的前提を多く共有している。〔このうち〕新現実主義の方がより有力である。その主張によれば，国家は国際システムの物質的な構造的インセンティブに従って行動する。国家の行動は，国際システム内部における各国家の地位を反映する。各国家の利益と戦略は，このシステムにおける自国の地位に関する計算に基づく。それゆえ，各国家はせめてこのシステムにおける自国の相対的な地位を維持しようとする。国家は，能力が大きければ大きいほど，国際的な権力ヒエラルキーの中で上位に位置し，国際舞台における影響力も大きくなる。国際システムの構造は，国家間におけるこの国力の分布によって定義される。国家の行動に対する新現実主義者の理解には，中心となる仮定が〔以下のように〕５つある。

1. 第一の，最も基本的な仮定は，無政府状態，すなわち国際システム内部に至上の権威が存在しないという仮定である。これは，国際協定を執行したり，国家の正当な利益を保護したりすることができる権力は，国家自体のほかには存在しないことを意味する。
2. 国家は軍事力を持ち，相互に危険な存在となりうる。一部の新現実主義者は，権力は軍事力に還元可能なものと考えている。
3. 国家は他の国家の意図を決して確実に知ることができない。ある日の同盟国は，次の日には敵になる可能性がある。
4. 国家の動機となるのは存続に対する関心である。
5. 国家は完璧無比な合理的行為者である。

無政府状態というのは，国家が常に安全保障や自国の存続の問題に没頭していなければならないということである。国家はただ自らのみを頼りとし，他の国家を恐れる。国家は，無政府状態が突き付ける要求に従って行為しないならば，結果的に弱体化する。この論理を用いて，新現実主義者は国際協力をきわめて実現困難なものとして説明する。国家は，協力関係から他の国家が自国よりも多くを得る場合，協力を避ける〔からである〕。

　新自由主義的制度主義は，新現実主義〔が掲げる〕ムダのない利己的な合理的行為者の仮定を用いようとする。それは，国際システム内部において無政府状態の下での協力が可能であることを示すためである。新自由主義者はこのような協力について，国際的な制度やレジームが無政府状態の影響を緩和する能力を持つことによって実現すると考える。新自由主義的制度主義者は，国家を合理的エゴイストであるとして記述する──すなわち，国家というものは自国の利益のみを追求するものであり，自らの効用を高めることにしか関心がない〔と考える〕。各国家は，自国の効用を計算する際に他国の効用関数にはほとんど関心を持たない。そのため，ある協力の取り組みが相互に有益であれば，その協力行動には加わる可能性がある。

　最後に，新自由主義者は一般に経済的相互作用にその理論を限定しており，安全保障面では協力のダイナミクスを実現することがはるかに困難だと考えていることに留意すべきである。大半の新自由主義者は，新現実主義がいう「無政府状態の国際システム」という性格付けを受け入れている。繰り返すが，無政府状態とは至上の権威がないことを示し，国家による国際協定の遵守を確保する執行メカニズムの欠如を意味している。したがって，新自由主義は国家間の協力を妨げる主要な障害として，不正行為や離脱に対する恐れを指摘する。この恐れゆえに，国家にとって相互の利益のために力を合わせることが合理的な場合でさえ，協力が妨げられるのである。

　制度やレジームは，3つの異なる方法でこの恐怖に対処する。第一に，制度やレジームは法的責任感（すなわち，国家間にある，ルールや協定遵守に対する義務感）を生み出す。第二に，国家間の取引コスト（問題領域内と問題領域間の相互関係のコスト，規則が破られた場合のコスト）を削減する。最後に，問題領域と国家の行動に関する透明性と情報を提供する。これがレジームの最も重要な機能である。レジームの全体的効果とは，システム内の不確実性を減少させることであり，それによって国家がより全面的に協力できるようになる。このように，レジームは無政府状態がもたらす影響を緩和するものである。新現実主義と新自由主義はいずれも，レジームを国家の手段として考究する。あるレジームの有効性は，そのレジームのルールを各国家が遵守する程度によって直接測られる。

<table>
<tr><td>VII</td><td>下線部の単語や句の意味を最もよく表しているものを
4つの選択肢の中から1つ選びなさい。</td></tr>
</table>

61.　解答：C

解説 commit to はこの場合「〜について約束する」の意。よって最も近いのは C.「実行を誓う」。

62.　解答：C

解説 原形 jeopardize は expose to danger or risk の意。よって最も近いのは C.「危険にさらす」。

63.　解答：B

解説 bumper はこの場合 exceptionally large の意。最も近いのは B.「巨大な」。

64.　解答：C

解説 原形の insist はこの場合 state positively and assertively を意味するので，最も近いのは C.「主張した」。

65.　解答：B

解説 review はこの場合，critical appraisal of a book, play, film, etc. published in a newspaper or magazine を意味する。B.「評価」が最も近い。

66.　解答：A

解説 mitigate には「（負の影響を）緩和する」の意味があるが，最も近いのは A.「（不快なもの，激烈なものを）和らげる，拡大を防ぐ」。

67.　解答：C

解説 原形の caution は say something as a warning の意。よって C.「予測（予言）する」が最も近い。

68.　解答：B

解説 in the face of は成句で when confronted with の意味だが，この文脈は

in the face of a warning planet であるから，「地球温暖化が予想される中」のような意味になる。

69. 解答：C

解説 これは基本的な単語。

70. 解答：D

解説 元の動詞 assessment が evaluate, estimate の意味を持つので，最も近いものとして D.「判断」が選べる。

訳例 国連は木曜日，気候変動に関連した侵食の被害を受けている地域に住む人が現在5億人以上いると警鐘を鳴らすとともに，手遅れになる前に温室効果ガスの排出を抑制する一助として，持続可能な土地利用に取り組むようすべての国々に促した。国連気候変動に関する政府間パネル（IPCC）の特別報告書『気候変動と土地』の発表会（開催地ジュネーブ）で専門家が〔発言し〕，肥沃な土壌に対する圧力の増大に関係する地球の気温上昇によって地球の食料安全保障が危険にさらされる恐れがあると強調した。

1,200ページに及ぶ大部の報告書に寄稿した3つの作業部会のうちの1部会で共同議長を務めるヴァレリー・マソン＝デルモット博士は，氷のない陸域については人間〔の利用〕による影響を受けているものが70%以上，すでに劣化したものが4分の1を占めると指摘した。同博士の報道陣への説明によると，「砂漠化が進行する地域に住む人は現在5億人で，すでに劣化した地域や砂漠化した地域に住む人々は，気候変動によるマイナスの影響をますます被っている」。この土壌劣化は，大地の炭素吸収可能量に直接影響を与えているという。

別の作業部会のジム・スキア共同議長は，世界8億2,000万人以上が栄養不足に陥っているという最近の各報告の中から，食品の損失および廃棄率が最大30%に達している事実を強調した。今後各国は，〔食品〕損失と廃棄の問題に取り組むあらゆる選択肢を検討し，それによって土地に対する圧力，それに伴う温室効果ガスの排出を減らすべきであり，〔その方法としては〕植物由来のいわゆる「バイオ」燃料〔原料植物〕の栽培も含まれる，と同氏は述べた。

博士は次のように主張した。「地球温暖化を摂氏1.5度，せめて2度に抑えるには，大気から二酸化炭素を除去する必要があるので，土地は二酸化炭素の除去に重要な役割を持つ。農作業は土壌に炭素を蓄積する助けとなるが，さらにまた，炭素の回収・貯留や森林の拡大を伴うか否かは別にして，バイオエネルギーの利用増加にもつながる」。

IPCC 報告書は，全世界 50 カ国以上の科学者 107 人によって作成されたもので（寄稿者の半数以上が途上国出身者），今日の土地利用に関する最新の研究をピアレビューしている。IPCC 報告書によると，農林業やその他の土地利用による温室効果ガス排出量は全体の約 4 分の 1 を占める。このことは，政策立案者が気候変動に適応し，その影響を緩和する投資のありかたを検討する際に考慮すべき点である。

第 2 作業部会のデブラ・ロバーツ共同議長は，「気温上昇を摂氏 2 度以下に抑えようとするならば，全部門の温室効果ガス排出量を削減することが絶対に必要だ」と述べた上で，「この目標を達成するために利用できるエネルギー作物や植林の規模には限界がある」と注意を促した。

また，温暖化する地球に対して早急な行動を取る必要性を強調したのは，別の作業部会の共同議長，ハンス＝オットー・ペルトナー氏。「『おや，気候変動が起きている。適応すれば（していけば）いい』などとは誰も言うことはできない。適応する能力は限られている〔からだ〕」と力を込めた。気候変動に関連した土地に対する圧力から多くの国が難題を抱えているが，積極的な行動がいま求められる，とペルトナー博士は断言した。世界人口が 2050 年には約 100 億人に達するとする予測を念頭に〔置いた発言である〕。

「脆弱性が極端に大きい地域や場所が一部にあり，特に緯度が低い地域に多いが，しかし，そのような国であっても，開発戦略において適応を重視している場合は，緩和が重要な役割を果たすことが望ましい」（同氏）。

報告書の原稿は，木曜日の発表に先立って 195 の加盟国による評価と承認が求められ，水曜日には予想以上の時間を要した。『土地関係特別報告書』に加え，IPCC では来月，国連気候行動サミット（9 月 23 日にニューヨークで開催）を前に，『変化する気候下での海洋・雪氷圏』に関する最新の知見〔IPCC『海洋・雪氷圏特別報告書』〕を発表する予定だ。

IPCC は，気候変動と予測しうる影響，将来の潜在リスクに関する定期的な科学的評価を政策立案者に提供し，適応および緩和戦略を提示する目的で，1988 年，国連環境計画（UNEP）と世界気象機関（WMO）により設立された。

VIII 文脈上，空所を埋めるのに最もふさわしいものを
4 つの選択肢の中から 1 つ選びなさい。

71. 解答：A

解説　原子力施設事故のニュースが流れはじめたときの状況を記述しているので，下線部前後は「当該地域の放射線量が上昇した」の意と推測できる。

72. 解答：D

解説　空所前後は「その日の朝に開いた電話会見で大統領報道官は報道陣に対

し，『残念ながら事故は起きるものだ』と述べた。_____，原子力の専門家と交渉担当者にとっては今回のこの事故が起こるべくして起こったような感覚があった」。このつながりから考えると，D.「確かに」が最適。

73. 解答：A
解説 センテンス頭に promised があり，空所はその「約束」の内容を同格の名詞節で表現していると考えると，A.「誓約」が適切。

74. 解答：B
解説 空所前後の意味は「〔ミサイル〕システムはかなり異例のもので，_____の準備完了に向けてそれほど進んでいるとか，準備完了に近いとは言えない」。したがって最適な語は B.「配備」。

75. 解答：C
解説 空所前後の意味は，「世界の安全保障構造を支える条約システムが過去数年の間に，ロシアと欧米の外交関係と軌を一にして_____してきているからである」。よって最適な語は C.「綻ぶ」。

76. 解答：B
解説 空所前後は「米国，ロシア，中国が開発を進めている戦略兵器の中で，どの軍縮条約にとっても_____ないまったく新たなタイプのものがある」。よって B.「対象となる」が最適。空所後の前置詞 to とのコロケーションにも着目する。

77. 解答：A
解説 空所後の意味は「ロシア国外ではいまのところ放射線レベルの上昇は検出されていない_____，北欧諸国の当局者は，破損した兵器が海を汚染し〜可能性があるとの懸念を表明している」。よって逆説の接続詞が選べる。

78. 解答：C
解説 空所前後は「1986 年のチェルノブイリ原子力発電所爆発事故では，ソ連

当局が事故発生後，数日待ってから地域からの避難を実施したため，何千人もの市民を異常に高いレベルの放射線に _____ した」の意。よって，C.「曝露する」が最適。

79.　解答：D

解説　空所前後は「ロシア市民は，世界の他の地域と同じく，セヴェロドヴィンスク市近郊で先週起きた爆発事故の被害の全容をまだ知らない。それを知るには時間がかかるし，ロシア政府が依然達成できていないレベルの _____ が必要になる」の意味。よって空所には D.「透明性」が最適。

80.　解答：A

解説　空所前後の意味は，「今日の軍拡競争のペースは加速しつつあり，この種の兵器の製造に対する法的制約も綻びを見せはじめている _____ ，こうした出来事はほぼ避けがたいように思われる」。よって，順接の接続詞 A. Given (that) を選ぶ。

訳例　　ロシア極北部の軍事基地で起きた核爆発の情報が少しずつ流れはじめた。

　当初は国営メディアの速報で，原因不明の事故で少なくとも2人が死亡したと伝えられた。その後，その地域で放射線量が急増したというニュースや，被害者を治療中の防護服を着た医師とされる映像が報道された。そしてついに8月13日，爆発から5日後にロシア政府が表に現れ，ウラジミル・プーチン大統領が持つ軍備の中でも最新部類の兵器に対して実施した試験の最中に核科学者5人のほか少なくとも2人が死亡したことを認めた。

　その日の朝に開いた電話会見で大統領報道官は報道陣に対し，「残念ながら事故は起きるものだ」と述べた。

　確かに，原子力の専門家と交渉担当者にとっては今回のこの事故が起こるべくして起こったかのような感覚があった。プーチン大統領は昨年の年次教書演説で世界に向けて新型核ミサイルの開発を宣言し，ロケットがフロリダにドーンと着弾する場面を描いたアニメーションを流して〔成功を〕誓った。しかし，大統領が誇らしげに語っていた核武装巡航ミサイルや放射性物質を搭載した水中無人機といった兵器は，製造が困難かつ危険であることがよく知られている。

　オバマ政権時に国家安全保障会議で軍備管理問題を担当した原子力専門家のリン・ラステン氏は次のように話している。「プーチンが公開の場で話していたシステムはかなり異例のもので，配備の準備完了に向けてそれほど進んでい

105

るとか，準備完了に近いとは言えない。だから米国はそういうものは追求しなかった」。

　少なくとも，これまではその通りだ。しかし，先週の爆発から学ぶべき1つの教訓は，ロシアでもアメリカでも中国でも，いずれの国もルールに違反することなくそうした兵器の開発を追求しうるということだろう。それはなぜかといえば，世界の安全保障構造を支える条約システムが過去数年の間に，ロシアと欧米の外交関係と軌を一にして綻びを見せてきたからである。

　米国は8月2日，ロシアが長年にわたって禁止兵器を配備していることを非難し，中距離核戦力（INF）全廃条約を正式に脱退した。同条約は1987年，両国の軍拡を抑止する目的で締結された。また，米ロ間で結ばれたさらに野心的な核軍縮条約（新START）が2021年に期限切れを迎えるが，延長される見通しは明るくない。プーチン大統領は6月，条約をさらに5年間延長する意向を示したが，トランプ〔政権〕のジョン・ボルトン国家安全保障担当大統領補佐官は，米国が応じる「可能性は低い」と述べている。

　その結果〔現れたのは〕核兵器に対する抑制が弱まるとともに，核兵器製造能力を持つ国が増していく世界である。新STARTの交渉に携わったゲリー・サモア氏はタイム誌の取材に対し，次のように話している。「いまは質の面での軍拡競争が進んでいる。米国，ロシア，中国が開発を進めている戦略兵器の中で，どの軍縮条約の対象にもならないまったく新しいタイプのものがある」。

　8月8日の爆発は，その新しい現実が孕む危険性を浮き彫りにしている。〔ロシアの〕国営通信社イタルタス通信は爆発について，ロシアの国営原子力機関ロザトムのスタッフ数名が試験場から吹き飛ばされ，白海に落とされるほどの威力があったと報じた。ロシア国外ではいまのところ放射線レベルの上昇は検出されていないが，北欧諸国の当局者は，破損した兵器が海を汚染し，市民に危険をもたらす可能性があるとの懸念を表明している。爆発現場に最も近いロシアの村に対して月曜日に避難命令が出されたとされるが，現地当局者はその翌日，避難は行われないと述べた。

　今回の爆発をめぐる秘密のベールから明らかになった核時代の不快な事実がもう1つある。それは，政府が最も危険な技術の取り扱いについて過ちを認めたがらず，そうした過ちを隠そうとする気持ちによって，その過ちがいっそう致命的なものとなった場合が多かった〔という事実だ〕。

　1986年のチェルノブイリ原子力発電所爆発事故では，ソ連当局が発生後，数日待って地域からの避難を実施したため，何千人もの市民が異常に高いレベルの放射線を被曝した。プーチン大統領の任期の最初の年となった2000年，ロシアの潜水艦クルスクがバレンツ海で沈没したが，大統領配下の司令官らは，同艦の核に関する秘密厳守にこだわるあまり，救助活動に対する外国の支援を数日にわたって拒否した。ノルウェーの潜水士が許可を得て艦内に入ったときには，乗組員118人全員が死亡していた。

ロシア市民は，世界の他の地域と同じく，セヴェロドヴィンスク市近郊で先週起きた爆発事故の被害の全容をまだ知らない。それを知るには時間がかかるし，ロシア政府が依然達成できていないレベルの透明性が必要になる。

　しかし，〔現在〕得られる詳細情報だけからでも，これが単なる不運ではなかったということは十分理解できる。今日の軍拡競争のペースは加速しつつあり，この種の兵器の製造に対する法的制約も綻びを見せはじめていることから，こうした出来事はほぼ避けがたいように思われる。

　かつて国防総省最高のロシア専門家であったマイケル・カーペンター氏は次のように話している。「我々は激烈な競争の時代に入りつつある。これに我々がいかに対処していくかということが，我々の国家安全保障にとってきわめて重要だ」。そして，核兵器管理の面では，そのいかんが世界の安全保障にとってきわめて重要となるのである。

IX 以下の質問に対し，150〜200語の短いエッセイを英語で書きなさい。

質問文：「ジェンダー平等は国連が世界において推進すべき中核目標であるが，それはなぜか？」

解答例　I will discuss three reasons why gender equality is central to the United Nations basic mission; these relate to UN history, present-day awareness of women's issues, and future plans as noted in the 2030 SDGs.

　Firstly, historically, the UN's founding document, the 1945 UN charter, begins with reaffirming "equal rights of men and women". Further, all agencies, boards, commissions, good works, affiliated organizations, missions and bodies associated with the UN must follow the inclusive standard the UN has been striving to live up to for the last 75 years.

　Secondly, news coverage and social media reportage of women's rights inadequacies nourishes current awareness of the urgent need for action to remedy all forms of discrimination against half the world's population. We increasingly understand issues interact to disadvantage females; drought and traditional female roles to get water for household needs prevent girls from attending school.

Globally, women able to gain marketable skills earn only 23 percent of what men earn doing the same work.

In conclusion, in great detail, UN Women's 2018 goal-by-goal examination of "Why Gender Equality Matters Across All SDGs" compellingly illustrates how each aspect of sustainable development is interwoven with and reliant on the achievement of gender equality.

解説　全体に，国連システムに関する正確な知識を織り交ぜつつ，意見や論評を述べるようにするとよい。

第1パラグラフでは主題を設定する。ここでは，与えられた主題のもとで論じる項目を3つ列挙している。

第2パラグラフでは，第1項目の国連の歴史について，国連憲章の重要な規定や，関連組織が従うべき基準を指摘している。

第3パラグラフでは，女性問題に関する現代の認識について，就学と就労の問題に着目する。

第4パラグラフでは，第3論点であるSDGsについて，国連女性機関が行った検討を取り上げ，持続可能な開発目標とジェンダー平等の密接な関わりを指摘して結論に代えている。

訳例　ジェンダー平等が国連の基本的使命の中心となっている3つの理由について考える。3つとは，国連の歴史，女性問題に対する現在の認識，2030年SDGsに示されている将来計画に関わるものである。

第一に，歴史的に見ると，国連の設立文書である1945年の国連憲章は冒頭で「男女の同権」を再確認している。さらに，国連に関係するあらゆる機関や理事会，委員会，慈善活動，関連団体，ミッション，組織体は，国連が過去75年にわたって遵守を心がけてきた包摂的な基準に従わなければならない。

第二に，女性の権利の不備についてのニュースやソーシャルメディアの報道は，世界人口の半分〔を占める女性〕に対するあらゆる形態の差別を是正する行動が緊急に必要であるとする現代の意識を育むものである。干ばつによって，また，家庭で必要な水を得る上で女性が伝統的に果たしてきた役割によって女子の就学が妨げられるなど，問題が相互に絡み合って女性を不利にしているとの理解がますます深まっている。世界的に見ても，市場性のある技能を習得できる女性の収入は，同じ仕事をしている男性のわずか23％にとどまっている。

結論を詳細に示すと，国連女性機関〔国連男女平等・女性の地位向上機関〕では「ジェンダー平等が全SDGs横断的に重要なのはなぜか」という問題について2018年に目標ごとの検討を実施したが，これによって，持続可能な開発の各側面がジェンダー平等の実現とどのように相互に絡み合い，それに依存し

ているかということが説得力をもって示された，と言えよう。

2019 年 A 級第 2 回試験　正解一覧

I
1. C　2. A　3. D　4. B　5. A　6. D　7. D　8. C　9. C　10. D

II
11. B　12. D　13. A　14. B　15. B　16. B　17. A　18. D　19. A　20. C

III
21. B　22. B　23. B　24. D　25. C　26. D　27. A　28. C　29. A　30. D

IV
31. B　32. A　33. C　34. C　35. B　36. D　37. A　38. D　39. B　40. C

V
41. D　42. A　43. B　44. C　45. D　46. A　47. D　48. A　49. C　50. A

VI
51. C　52. A　53. D　54. C　55. C　56. D　57. C　58. A　59. C　60. D

VII
61. C　62. C　63. B　64. C　65. B　66. A　67. C　68. B　69. C　70. D

VIII
71. A　72. D　73. A　74. B　75. C　76. B　77. A　78. C　79. D　80. A

110

2020年

第2回試験

問題

A級

外務省後援

２０２０年度第２回国際連合公用語

英語検定試験（120分）

受験上の注意

1. 問題用紙は試験開始の合図があるまで開いてはいけません。その間に、この**受験上の注意を熟読**しておいてください。

2. **受験番号と氏名を解答用紙（マークシートと作文用紙）に記入してください。**

3. 解答用紙の配布は１人１部のみです。複数の配布は致しません。

4. 試験開始前は、答案への解答記入は禁止です。

5. マークシートの記入は、１～100までの記入箇所がありますが、この級では１～80までを使います。

6. マークシートの記入は、必ずＨＢ以上の濃い鉛筆を使って該当箇所を黒く塗りつぶしてください。書き間違いの場合は「アト」が残らないように消してください。マークシートは絶対に折ったり曲げたりしないでください。

7. 受験級、受験地区、会場番号、受験番号のマークシートへの記入は監督者の指示に従い、間違いなく記入してください。（裏表紙の「マークシート記入例」参照）

8. 作文は、⑴読みやすい文字をペン、ボールペンまたはＨＢ以上の濃い鉛筆で書いてください。⑵使用語数の150～200語を目安にしてください。

9. 試験問題についての質問は、印刷が不鮮明な場合を除き、一切受けつけません。

10. 中途退室の際は、マークシートと作文用紙を持って監督者に渡し、他の受験者の迷惑にならないように静かに退室してください。中途退室後の再入室はできません。

11. 試験中は他の受験者の妨げとなる行動は慎んでください。また携帯電話等の電源はお切りください。

12. マークシートと作文用紙は監督者に提出し、問題用紙はご自由にお持ち帰りください。

＊試験問題の複製や転載、インターネットへのアップロード等、いかなる媒体への転用を禁止します。

試験結果について

1. 第１次試験の結果は2020年11月25日㈬頃に受験申込書に記載された住所に郵送で通知します。

2. その間に住所変更をされた方は、郵便局へ住所変更の届け出を忘れずに行ってください。

3. 発表前の試験結果のお問合せには応じられません。

第２次試験について

1. 第１次試験合格者には、試験結果発表と同時に試験日時、会場を指定して通知します。（第１次試験を特別会場で受験した合格者には最寄りの２次試験会場が指定されます。）

2. 第２次試験は2020年12月13日㈰です。A級の試験地は札幌・仙台・東京・名古屋・大阪・福岡・鹿児島・沖縄のいずれかになります。（特A級との併願で特A級の第１次試験に合格された方の試験地は東京と大阪になります。）あらかじめご了承願います。

公　益
財団法人　日本国際連合協会

http://www.unaj.or.jp/

I. Fill in each of the following blanks with the most appropriate of the four alternatives according to the knowledge and information gained from *New Today's Guide to the United Nations*.

1. **Basic Facts about the United Nations**
   The United Nations proper is composed of six principal organs: the General Assembly, the Security Council, the Economic and Social Council, the Trusteeship Council, the International Court of Justice and the _____.
   A. Administrative Bureau   B. Secretariat
   C. Committee   D. Liaison Office

2. **Name of the United Nations**
   The name "United Nations" was suggested by United States President Franklin D. Roosevelt. It was first used officially in 1942, when representatives of _____ countries signed the Declaration by the United Nations, pledging their cooperation in the "struggle for victory over Hitlerism."
   A. 10   B. 14
   C. 23   D. 26

3. **Official Languages**
   United Nations staff members speak some 170 languages. To avoid a Babel of tongues in the Organization, a handful of languages have been designated as "official" or "_____" languages.
   A. common   B. general
   C. working   D. formal

4. **General Assembly**
   The General Assembly meets once a year in regular session, commencing on _____ in September and continuing until mid-December.
   A. the third Thursday   B. the second Thursday
   C. the third Tuesday   D. the first Tuesday

5. **Economic and Social Council**
   The Economic and Social Council generally holds one substantive session each year. This annual session used to alternate between New York and _____, but now is held only in New York every year, with the exception of the Humanitarian Affairs Segment.
   A. Geneva   B. Vienna
   C. Paris   D. Rome

6. **Human Rights Council**

The Human Rights Council comprises _____ Member States elected by the General Assembly, representing a geographically fair distribution of seats. The Council members shall pledge to contribute to the promoting and protecting of human rights. These elected members shall uphold the highest standards in the promotion and protection of human rights.

A. 5   B. 12

C. 23   D. 47

7. **ILO**

The International Labour Organization (ILO) was established in 1919 as an autonomous institution associated with the _____ of Nations.

A. Federation   B. League

C. Association   D. Community

8. **UNESCO**

Owing to the increase of member countries from newly independent countries beginning the 1960s, UNESCO developed more _____ policies, aggravating conflict with the United States.

A. detailed   B. stringent

C. independent   D. integrated

9. **IMF**

In order to prevent the re-introduction of exchange control and discriminatory _____, the 1944 Bretton Woods Conference discussed the international economic order to be formed for the postwar world and drew up the Articles of Agreement of the International Monetary Fund (IMF).

A. treatments   B. policies

C. prices   D. tariffs

10. **UN Diplomacy in the Early Days and the East-West, South-North Confrontations**

Japan's admission to the UN in _____ as its 80th member coincided with the so-called detente that had eased the tension between the East and West camps.

A. 1951   B. 1953

C. 1956   D. 1960

II. **Choose from among the four alternatives the one that is the most appropriate form of each of the underlined verbs.**

Zimbabwe has quietly lifted a ban on imports of genetically modified corn for the first time in 12 years as the southern African nation **(11) begin** to take action to avert what could be its worst famine.

While genetically modified corn imports from South Africa are being allowed, the grain is carefully quarantined and is milled into a corn meal, a national staple, three officials with knowledge of the situation said, **(12) ask** not to be identified as an announcement has not been made. Currently corn meal, used to make the staple food known locally as sadza, is in short supply across the nation.

Zimbabwe is battling its worst drought in 40 years and is in the midst of an economic collapse. That's **(13) leave** about 8 million people, or more than half the population, in need of food aid.

Aside from in South Africa, genetically modified corn is shunned across sub-Saharan Africa and in Zimbabwe steps are being taken to ensure the grain **(14) not enter** national seed stocks. A logistics team has been sent to South Africa to have oversight of the grain-import exercise, one of the people said. Plans are also under way to provide special clearance for trucks **(15) bring** in grain to avoid delays at southern Africa's busiest border, Beitbridge between South Africa and Zimbabwe.

Agriculture Minister Perence Shiri and the permanent secretary in the ministry, John Basera, didn't immediately respond to messages and phone calls **(16) seek** comment. Tafadzwa Musarara, chairman of the Grain Millers Association of Zimbabwe, also didn't respond to messages and calls.

"Government weighs its position on genetically modified corn against the nutritional needs of the nation **(17) proceed** guided by that assessment," said Nick Mangwana, the government's main spokesman, without saying whether the ban has been lifted.

The country's corn harvest is expected to plunge by more than half this season and there is a likely supply deficit of between 800,000 tons and 1 million tons.

Weekly imports of white corn, the variety used mainly for human consumption in the country, reached their highest in almost seven years, with 13,688 tons **(18) import** in the week ending Jan. 24.

The millers association on Jan. 22 said it had signed up for a monthly supply of 100,000 tons of corn from South Africa. Until now there has been little evidence of sufficient corn imports coming into the country.

Jannie de Villiers, chief executive officer at Grain SA, said it was possible for genetically modified corn to be separated **(19) send** straight for processing and Zimbabwe had done this previously.

"Historically, Zimbabwe only imports genetically modified-free corn, not because of food safety concerns, but seed safety concerns. Strategically, they do not want to be dependent

2020年
第2回
問題

115

on seed from multinational companies," de Villiers said in an emailed response to questions.

The industry and commerce ministry has 65 registered millers **(20) sign** up for its corn-subsidy program, which the government rolled out in December last year and is meant to provide affordable cornmeal.

11.   A.   was beginning   B.   had begun
        C.   that began   D.   begins

12.   A.   asked   B.   when asked
        C.   but asks   D.   asking

13.   A.   to leave   B.   leaving
        C.   left   D.   been left

14.   A.   wasn't entered   B.   doesn't enter
        C.   didn't enter   D.   hasn't entered

15.   A.   bring   B.   that brings
        C.   bringing   D.   brought

16.   A.   seeking   B.   but sought
        C.   were sought   D.   sought

17.   A.   proceed   B.   proceeding
        C.   proceeded   D.   and proceeds

18.   A.   imported   B.   importing
        C.   import   D.   to import

19.   A.   and sent   B.   but to send
        C.   by sending   D.   if sent

20.   A.   for signing   B.   that have signed
        C.   signed   D.   to be signed

Ⅲ. Fill in each of the following blanks with the most grammatically and logically appropriate of the four alternatives.

The head of the World Health Organization (WHO) appealed on Wednesday for $675 million **(21)** _____ epidemic, as deaths from the outbreak neared 500.

Speaking in Geneva, Tedros Adhanom Ghebreyesus said that latest data indicated 24,363 confirmed infections in China and 490 deaths from the respiratory disease (COVID-19), which was declared on 31 December. "In the last 24 hours, we had the **(22)** _____ _____ started (3925 new cases globally)," he said.

Noting the concern generated by the virus, Tedros added that "we must not forget how difficult it is for the people of Wuhan", in reference to the city at the epicentre of the outbreak in central China.

Outside China, 191 cases have been reported in 24 countries and there has been one death in the Philippines, the WHO Director-General told journalists. Of that number, 31 cases are people with no travel history to China, he explained, but **(23)** _____ _____ cases, or to someone from the hotspot city of Wuhan, where the epidemic originated.

This "relatively small number" of infections outside China — which is home to 99 per cent of cases, with 80 per cent of these in Hubei province alone — has presented a "window of opportunity" to **(24)** _____, the WHO Director-General insisted.

2020年
第2回
問題

Highlighting that the UN health agency's major concern is that the virus could reach countries without the capacity to detect infections, Mr. Tedros urged the international community to show solidarity — political, technical and financial — to ensure that it does not spread further.

"My biggest worry is that there are countries today who do not have the **(25)** __ _____ the virus, even if it were to emerge", he said. "Urgent support is needed to bolster weak health systems to detect, diagnose and care for people with the virus, to prevent further human to human transmission and protect health workers."

"We are only as strong as our weakest link", he said, adding that the WHO has released $9 million from its emergency financial reserves to help combat the epidemic. In addition, WHO has distributed some 500,000 facemasks, along with 350,000 medical gloves, 40,000 respiratory kits and around 18,000 isolation gowns to 24 countries.

The agency has also sent some 250,000 test samples to more than 70 laboratories around the world to speed up virus detection. "But we need to do more", he said, before outlining how the $675 million strategic preparedness and response appeal would support countries to protect their populations with better prevention measures and speedier diagnosis.

117

"We understand that people are worried and concerned, and rightly so," he said. "But this is not a time for fear. This is not a time for panic. It's is a time for rational, evidence-based action and **(26)** _____
to bring this outbreak under control."

To date there is no proven drug to treat the coronavirus, Dr Michael Ryan, Executive Director, WHO Health Emergencies Programme, told journalists. Confirming that a small WHO team of international epidemiology experts was expected to visit China "to learn from Chinese counterparts", Dr Ryan noted that the infection predominantly affects older patients with pre-existing conditions.

"Providing respiratory support (to affected individuals) is very important," he added, noting that while some deaths were linked to multiple organ failure, **(27)** _____
_____ timely care. The WHO believes that the outbreak poses a "very high" risk in China and a high risk regionally and globally.

Its risk assessment **(28)** _____
____ spread, the potential impact on human health, and the varying levels of effectiveness in national preparedness and response measures. Accelerated action, as called for in Wednesday's appeal, can address these risks and areas requiring support, the agency said in a statement.

The UN Food and Agriculture Organization (FAO), the International Fund for Agricultural Development (IFAD) and the World Food Programme (WFP) wrote to the Chinese premier on Wednesday, jointly **(29)** _____
_____ the outbreak.

In a joint letter to President Xi Jinping, the heads of the three agencies — FAO Director-General QU Dongyu, President of IFAD Gilbert Houngbo, and WFP Executive Director David Beasley — paid tribute to the resilience of the Chinese people and praised the efforts made by the country dealing with the emergency.

Describing the outbreak as a "health challenge for China and the rest of the world," the three Rome-based agencies pledged readiness to provide support, based on their respective areas of expertise, to China's **(30)** _____
_____ its population, particularly in rural areas.

21.　A.　measures to boost new coronavirus international to counter the
　　　B.　to counter international measures to boost the coronavirus new
　　　C.　new coronavirus boost to counter international measures to the
　　　D.　to boost international measures to counter the new coronavirus

22.　A.　day since the single cases in outbreak a most
　　　B.　most cases in a single day since the outbreak
　　　C.　outbreak since a single day in the most cases
　　　D.　single outbreak since the most cases in a day

23.
  A. all of them are close to contacts of confirmed
  B. close to them of confirmed all are contacts of
  C. contacts of them are close to confirmed of all
  D. them are close to of all of confirmed contacts

24.
  A. developing global crisis into a prevent the outbreak from
  B. from developing the global crisis into prevent outbreak a
  C. outbreak prevent the developing from into a crisis global
  D. prevent the outbreak from developing into a global crisis

25.
  A. people who have place in systems contracted to detect
  B. place who have contracted systems to detect people in
  C. systems in place to detect people who have contracted
  D. contracted people to detect systems in place who have

26.
  A. investment while we still have a window of opportunity
  B. opportunity of investment while a window we still have
  C. we still have a window of opportunity while investment
  D. while we have still opportunity of investment a window

27.
  A. patients survive very sick if they will sufficient receive
  B. sick patients will receive very sufficient if they survive
  C. sufficient will survive if they receive very sick patients
  D. very sick patients will survive if they receive sufficient

28.
  A. of further likelihood factors is based on the including
  B. including likelihood further is based on factors of the
  C. is based on factors including the likelihood of further
  D. on the likelihood including further factors is based of

29.
  A. and expressing solidarity support as the country battles offering
  B. expressing solidarity and offering support as the country battles
  C. offering battles expressing solidarity and the country as support
  D. support offering solidarity battles expressing as the country and

30.
  A. efforts to alleviate the impact of the virus on
  B. impact on the alleviate efforts to the virus of
  C. to alleviate the efforts of impact on the virus
  D. virus on the efforts of the impact to alleviate

119

Choose from among the four alternatives the one that best completes the following sentence.

31. Brexit is a _____ for the United Kingdom. Given the risk that it will now lose Scotland and Northern Ireland to _____, the country seems to have accepted the idea of Great Britain turning back into "Little England."
    A. disaster – secession
    B. calamity – foreclosure
    C. blow – integration
    D. setback – litigation

32. Along with climate shocks, conflict and _____ food insecurity, the East Africa region now faces a hunger threat from desert locusts, top UN relief officials warned on Tuesday, saying action now will _____ a major food crisis later.
    A. dire – induce
    B. lavish – confront
    C. sporadic – thwart
    D. acute – avert

33. North Korea's possession of an arsenal of nuclear-_____ missiles increasingly looks permanent. The U.S. government will continue to refuse to officially recognize this reality, mostly out of deference to Tokyo. However, the region has settled into a new _____.
    A. powered – disagreement
    B. armed – status quo
    C. equipped – procedure
    D. capable – era

34. Independent UN human rights experts on Tuesday voiced grave concern _____ the killing and displacement of civilians in north-west Myanmar during the intensifying conflict between the military and an armed group, the Arakan Army, _____ an information blackout in some parts of Rakhine and Chin states.
    A. about – despite
    B. from – to
    C. over – amid
    D. between – for

35. For 70 years, India has struggled to remain a _____ state. In spite of its people being overwhelmingly Hindu, it chose not to distinguish between its citizens — or putative citizens — _____ their religion.
    A. democratic – in spite of
    B. autocratic – with reference to
    C. secular – on the basis of
    D. schismatic – given

36. With progress _____ on both the peace and political fronts in Syria, UN Special Envoy Geir Pedersen urged ambassadors in the Security Council on Wednesday to "put their _____ " into finding a solution to end nearly nine years of conflict.
   A. stalled − weight   B. spurred − end
   C. reinstituted − faith   D. expedited − stress

37. Following a U.S.-Turkey presidential telephone conversation the night before, U.S. troops _____ in northern Syria started to withdraw from the region on Oct. 7. Within less than 48 hours, Ankara began its military _____ into the Kurdish region there.
   A. fortified − offensive   B. stationed − incursion
   C. deployed − sway   D. mutilated − operation

38. The UN High Commissioner for Human Rights, Michelle Bachelet, on Friday denounced the "high human cost" of the recent _____ in Ecuador and urged all actors in the South American country to engage in dialogue to prevent new conflicts and forge an _____ society "with full respect for its multicultural nature".
   A. turmoil − dedicated   B. skirmish − prosperous
   C. havoc − irreconcilable   D. unrest − inclusive

39. It posted tens of thousands of troops in Iraq, _____ with its leaders and helped craft its laws — but with the country swamped by deadly protests, Washington is staying out of the _____.
   A. bickered − chaos   B. huddled − fray
   C. collaborated − detention D. colluded − adversity

40. Japan, the United States and the European Union on Tuesday proposed expanding a ban on market-_____ subsidies under World Trade Organization rules, a measure _____ targeted at China.
   A. distorting − apparently   B. driven − leniently
   C. oriented − ostensibly   D. manipulating − poignantly

121

V. Choose from among the underlined phrases the one that is grammatically or idiomatically incorrect.

41. The National Institute of Infectious Diseases **(A)** <u>said Friday that it has succeeded</u> **(B)** <u>in cultivating and isolated the</u> new coronavirus, **(C)** <u>first reported in the Chinese city of</u> Wuhan, from a person **(D)** <u>in Japan who has been confirmed to</u> have the virus.

42. **(A)** <u>Once Australia's "catastrophic" and</u> deadly wildfire emergency continues, UN weather **(B)** <u>experts on Tuesday echoed government</u> **(C)** <u>warnings for</u> people to remain vigilant in **(D)** <u>the face of the fast-moving threat and</u> tinderbox conditions.

43. Prime Minister Shinzo Abe **(A)** <u>has, so far, managed keeping the</u> outbreak of new coronavirus COVID-19 **(B)** <u>from damaging his hard-won relationship with</u> China, **(C)** <u>but that's getting more difficult</u> **(D)** <u>with each new case confirmed</u> in Japan.

44. The U.S. State Department on Wednesday **(A)** <u>mourned the loss of</u> Sadako Ogata, a former United Nations high commissioner for refugees, **(B)** <u>saying that her legacy of</u> **(C)** <u>an advocate for displaced persons</u> **(D)** <u>is an "inspiration" to</u> humanitarian workers worldwide.

45. The UN Secretary-General António Guterres **(A)** <u>has expressed deep concern over the</u> **(B)** <u>latest escalation in tension across</u> the Gulf region, **(C)** <u>following the killing of a top</u> Iranian General in Iraq, in **(D)** <u>an airstrike was carried out by</u> the United States.

46. **(A)** <u>Despite a global progress in</u> tackling poverty, hunger and disease, a "new generation **(B)** <u>of inequalities" indicates that</u> many societies **(C)** <u>are not working as they</u> should, the UN Development Programme (UNDP) **(D)** <u>argues in</u> its latest report released on Monday.

47. The Japanese government has officially determined that environment minister Shinjiro Koizumi's **(A)** <u>recent use of the</u> English word "sexy" **(B)** <u>in a reference to climate change is</u> "difficult **(C)** <u>to accurate translate" into</u> Japanese, **(D)** <u>avoiding issuing an official rendering of</u> the young scion's tricky choice of vocabulary.

122

48. Japan and South Korea (**A**) <u>took fresh swipes at one another</u> Sunday, (**B**) <u>raising questions about whether relations</u> (**C**) <u>between the U.S.</u> allies would <u>improve after</u> they (**D**) <u>reached to a last-minute deal Friday to rescue an expiring</u> intelligence-sharing pact.

49. (**A**) <u>New data published by the</u> United Nations cultural agency on Friday, (**B**) <u>reveals that without taking</u> urgent measures, around 12 million (**C**) <u>young children would never have set foot</u> (**D**) <u>inside a school, with girls facing</u> "the greatest barriers".

50. (**A**) <u>In a bid to scale up</u> investment efforts to reach sustainable development targets, the Secretary-General on Wednesday (**B**) <u>convened the first meeting of a</u> new UN-backed corporate alliance (**C**) <u>to discuss plans for spending on</u> (**D**) <u>sustainability, is likely to be in the</u> trillions of dollars.

VI. Choose from among the four alternatives the one that most closely corresponds to the meaning of words in bold type and blanks in the following passage.

I'd spent the past 10 years in Washington, D.C., trying to make a difference. Lots of folks said that my call to politics was like a call to the priesthood: that I was meant for it. It started in 2000, when I did get a call, but it wasn't from God or even from Washington, D.C.—it was from my mother. She told me the doctors had found a lump in her breast, and that the diagnosis was breast cancer. Because my father had retired, my mother was ineligible for Medicare and my father would have to **(51)** _____ retirement so that my mother could have affordable access to healthcare.

I, the bright-eyed twenty-something, thought I'd do something about it. Years and a war in Iraq later, I found myself driving up to Burlington, Vermont, to work for Governor Howard Dean. I'd never voted before, but Dean was a medical doctor, and had **(52) made reasonable moves on** healthcare in his home state. He was the only person running for president who seemed like he could get my mother's health insurance premiums down, and make it so my dad could retire again. That started my career in politics. But it became obvious that I wasn't solving the problem that I'd set out to solve. After electing a majority of Democrats to the House in 2006 and still seeing no movement on healthcare, I decided that electing Democrats to fix the problem wasn't doing a whole lot of good. There must have been some other **(53)** _____ I needed to address.

I took a new job at the Sunlight Foundation and was directing a squad of technologists. Our mission was to liberate and analyze government data, and to make it easier for people to make more informed decisions about elections. If we could show America with hard facts that their Congress was being bought off, surely that would **(54) spur** them to action. After two years on the job at Sunlight—a full eight years since my mom was diagnosed—I watched the newly-elected President Barack Obama bring up healthcare. It should have been a great moment, the realization of my hopes for nearly a decade. **(55)** _____, I watched the nation go into a bitter and angry debate about the role of our government.

The news media was saturated with every kind of graph and chart about our healthcare costs, wait times, the efficiency of government, how Canada does it, how old people handle healthcare, and what kinds of medicines would and would not be available to Americans should we pass some form of healthcare overhaul. At Sunlight, we did our best to **(56) stick to** the facts. We built "Sunlight Live," which allowed people to watch the healthcare debates online; next to each member of Congress when they spoke appeared the amount of money they had received from the healthcare industry.

During that long, bitter, and angry debate, I took a stroll down to the White House. And that's when I saw that sign, those jarring seven words, held high: "Keep your government hands off my Medicare." I spoke to this protestor about his sign. He seemed rather well educated—sure, he was angry, but he was not dumb. This man did not suffer from a lack of information. Yet he had failed to consider the **(57)** _____ of holding a sign above his head asking government to keep its hands off a government-run program. To him, it made perfect sense. **(58)** _____ could it be possible that educated, intelligent people have somehow become capable of believing in a distorted reality? At that moment, an idea popped into my head. What if a person's native or learned abilities to process information sensibly could be **(59) warped** by feeding junk into the mental machine?

We know we're products of the food we eat. Why wouldn't we also be products of the information we consume? If unhealthy information consumption creates bad information habits the way unhealthy eating creates food addictions, then what good is transparency? I left the Sunlight Foundation. Transparency wasn't the answer I was looking for. If large numbers of people only seek out information that confirms their beliefs, **(60)** _____ the market with data from and about the government will really not work as well as the theorists predict; the data ends up being twisted by the left- and right-wing political machines, and turned into more garbage to keep America spinning.

51.   **From the context, the underlined blank could best be filled with**
    A.   allow for   B.   come out of
    C.   make the best of   D.   take off

52.   **In this context, "made reasonable moves on" is closest in meaning to**
    A.   accepted a partial loss   B.   established a sensible precedent
    C.   slightly changed position   D.   taken some action

53.   **From the context, the underlined blank could best be filled with**
    A.   complaint   B.   criticism
    C.   impediment   D.   inhibition

54.   **From the context, "spur" is best replaced by**
    A.   boost   B.   incite
    C.   lift   D.   revitalize

55.   **From the context, the underlined blank could best be filled with**
    A.   As such   B.   Instead
    C.   Hence   D.   Like that

56.   **In this context, "stick to" is closest in meaning to**
    A.   abide by   B.   flout
    C.   prop up   D.   unearth

57. **From the context, the underlined blank could best be filled with**
A. irony
B. mockery
C. ridicule
D. sarcasm

58. **From the context, the underlined blank could best be filled with**
A. As a consequence,
B. Equally,
C. How
D. When

59. **In this context, "warped" is best replaced by**
A. buckled
B. distorted
C. crippled
D. perverted

60. **From the context, the underlined blank could best be filled with**
A. corrupting
B. empowering
C. flooding
D. liberating

VII. Choose from among the four alternatives the one that best explains each of the underlined words in the context of the article below.

The second global Ocean Conference taking place in Portugal in a few months' time promises to be "a **(61) critical** moment" for the health of life under water and on land, the President of the UN General Assembly said on Tuesday, as preparations got underway.

"Life under water is essential to life on land", said Tijjani Muhammad-Bande. The ocean produces "half of the oxygen we breathe" and provides food for millions of people around the world, playing a "fundamental role in **(62) mitigating** climate change as a major heat and carbon sink".

The Ocean Conference, which will run in Lisbon from 2 to 6 June, aims to **(63) propel** science-based innovative solutions in the form of global ocean action. The worldwide ocean economy is valued at around $1.5 trillion dollars annually, as aquaculture is the fastest growing food sector and 350 million jobs world-wide are linked to fisheries.

"A healthy marine environment holds untold potential for achieving the entirety of the Sustainable Development Agenda", he said. "Yet the unsustainable use — and misuse — of ocean resources, climate change, and pollution all threaten the ability of our ocean to provide for us all".

In this first year of the Decade of Action and Delivery, **(64) acceleration** is needed on the Sustainable Development Goal (SDGs) targets that are due to be met this year, two-thirds of which relate to the health of our environment.

Mr. Muhammad-Bande spelled out: "We must reach several targets related to SDG 14: Life Under Water to **(65) reframe** our understanding of nature as an accelerator for implementing the 2030 Agenda".

Life under water and on land have a "**(66) symbiotic** relationship", he said, noting that "pollution hampers the ocean's ability to provide for people". He referred to last year's UN Environment Assembly's ministerial declaration calling for a reduction of single-use plastic products by 2030 as demonstrating "multilateral commitment to forging a better world" and maintained the importance of **(67) emulating** this leadership at the Ocean Conference "to ensure that the declaration has a transformative impact on life under water".

While coral reefs are home to a quarter of all marine life, half have been lost, adversely impacting global food security. And illegal, unreported and unregulated fishing further burdens ecosystems. Moreover, sea level rise induced by climate-change poses an existential threat, with small island developing States at the frontline.

"We must stand with them in solidarity and support. This is for us all", the Assembly President stated, further emphasizing improving ocean health as "key to safeguarding our future".

(68) Transition toward a green economy is "essential to protect our oceans and our world", he said, recalling that next year marks the beginning of the Decade of Ocean Science for Sustainable Development.

127

Peter Thomson, Special Envoy for the Ocean, and himself a former President of the General Assembly, outlined five major problems facing the oceans. Pollution — from plastics to industrial agricultural sewerage — and the sustainability of fisheries in the face of harmful practices, are both "eminently fixable by 2030". However, more difficult to fix are problems associated with acidification, deoxygenation and ocean warming, all of which are linked to greenhouse gas emissions.

"We find ourselves in a much longer fixing period when it comes to those three", he said, noting that although they would continue for hundreds of years "even if we do the right thing tomorrow", indeed we must start doing [the right thing tomorrow], so "we can start turning the corner".

Mr. Thomson urged everyone to focus on the "positive tipping points", claiming they "are closer than you think". These include "scaling up of science and innovation" and other solutions "that we will be concentrating on in Lisbon", he elaborated. The UN envoy spoke about the "strong will" of developing countries to participate in sustainable agriculture, wind farms and the greening of shipping, stating that "we are now on the (69) **cusp** of a great positive revolution".

And speaking at a press conference for correspondents in New York, UN chief António Guterres highlighted the importance of oceans to the on-going climate crisis, and solutions to (70) **alleviate** it. He explained that "as oceans warm, ice melts and we lose the vital service the ice sheets perform — reflecting sunlight, thus further increasing ocean warming". And, as ice melts and the oceans warm, sea levels rise and more water evaporates, "fueling ever greater rainfall, threatening coastal cities and deltas".

The UN chief pointed out that last year, ocean heat and mean-sea level reached "their highest on record", revealing that scientists now say "that ocean temperatures are now rising at the equivalent of five Hiroshima bombs a second".

61. **critical**

A. dire   B. jocular

C. flippant   D. waggish

62. **mitigating**

A. proclaiming   B. patenting

C. palliating   D. promoting

63. **propel**

A. retard   B. advance

C. impede   D. hinder

64. **acceleration**
    A. hesitancy
    B. vacillation
    C. vindictiveness
    D. hastening

65. **reframe**
    A. restrain
    B. resist
    C. reevaluate
    D. renounce

66. **symbiotic**
    A. autonomous
    B. detached
    C. sovereign
    D. reciprocal

67. **emulating**
    A. contravening
    B. desecrating
    C. replicating
    D. violating

68. **Transition**
    A. Evolution
    B. Fixity
    C. Immobility
    D. Stasis

69. **cusp**
    A. bottom
    B. edge
    C. finale
    D. top

70. **alleviate**
    A. aggravate
    B. exacerbate
    C. infuriate
    D. moderate

VIII. Fill in each of the following blanks with the most appropriate of the four alternatives as required by the context.

A case brought to Colombia's top court by anti-abortion campaigner Natalia Bernal Cano could **(71)** _____ the country's abortion law when the verdict is announced in the next few weeks — but perhaps not in the way she hoped.

Since a 2006 ruling by Colombia's powerful Constitutional Court, women have been allowed to terminate a pregnancy in cases of rape or incest, fatal fetal abnormality, or danger to the physical or mental health of the mother.

Those three exceptions put Colombia in a middle-of-the-road position among Latin American and Caribbean countries' exceptionally strict regimes on abortion. Six countries in the region, including El Salvador and the Dominican Republic, ban all abortions, whatever the circumstances. Only Uruguay, Cuba and Guyana allow all **(72)** _____ abortions in early pregnancy.

Last year Bernal, a lawyer, filed two legal actions in the Constitutional Court, hoping to push Colombia back into the former camp. She argues that the three exceptions are unconstitutional, on the **(73)** _____ that all abortions carry health risks "for both the woman and her unborn child".

But one of the nine judges examining the case, Alejandro Linares Cantillo, argued that the court should consider why abortion is illegal in the first place. On Feb. 19 he issued a formal proposal for the other judges to consider legalizing all abortions in the first 16 weeks of pregnancy.

Between them, Linares and Bernal have revived a tense debate in Colombia, where almost three quarters of the population are Catholic. The ruling, expected by early March, will be closely watched in Colombia, and the rest of Latin America.

Opponents of abortion say Colombian authorities have become too **(74)** _____ about the procedure since 2006. Conservative politicians expressed outrage at the case of a woman in the western city of Popayán, who had a legal abortion in January at seven months pregnant as a result of mental-health problems.

The woman's ex-boyfriend, who had not wanted her to get an abortion, **(75)** _____ a widely reported campaign against her decision, staging protests and later threatening to sue her.

Bernal argues that exceptions like the one used by the woman in Popayán "cause **(76)** _____ harm to the people of Colombia," she told national newspaper El Espectador, including "post-traumatic stress" and "serious depressions" for women who have abortions.

Bernal has issued several unsuccessful requests for Linares to be recused for the case, arguing the judge, known for liberal leanings, is biased.

Abortion-rights groups say the Popayán case is an illustration of how hard it is to even get a legal abortion. Family-planning nonprofit Profamilia said the woman had been seeking a termination since her first trimester, but health officials refused her. The organization says 94% of women who seek an abortion do so within the first 15 weeks of pregnancy.

Paula Avila Guillen, a human rights lawyer and the Latin America director at the New York–based Women's Equality Center, says the current law discriminates against "poorer women who rely on the public health system" where the three-exceptions law is patchily implemented, while rich women can access abortions more easily from private doctors.

(77) _____ argue that legalizing all abortions in Colombia would prevent women from facing lengthy bureaucratic delays and free them from fear of arrest or prosecution if they seek medical help; data released by Colombia's attorney general last year showed that between 2005 and 2017, 2,290 women were (78) _____ for having an abortion — including 502 minors.

The court is unlikely to reverse the 2006 decision, local media report, since it has already upheld the constitutionality of the three exceptions on several occasions.

But it's less clear what the outcome will be for Linares' proposal for legal abortions up to 16 weeks. According to daily El Tiempo, four of the nine judges, including Linares, are likely to support the proposition and three are likely to oppose it. The two judges that are most likely to be swing votes are both women, according to Guillen.

(79) _____ a wave of protests across the region in recent years, no Latin American country has legalized abortion since Uruguay in 2012. Argentine activists' attempt to pass a legalization law failed in 2018, when the senate narrowly rejected the bill after the lower house approved it. Argentine legislators who support abortion are expected to try again soon, after new president Alberto Fernandez vowed to legalize abortion during his term.

Guillen says the last three years have felt like a turning point for abortion rights in the region. "It feels like we are taking back control and starting to move forward again, after a lull." The verdict in Colombia could turn the tide, she says, particularly if Bernal's attempt to reverse liberalization (80) _____. "With abortion debates all over the region, that would be a very good precedent to have."

| 71. | A. | retain | B. | galvanize |
| | C. | precipitate | D. | transform |

| 72. | A. | myriad | B. | elective |
| | C. | botched | D. | indulgent |

| 73. | A. | grounds | B. | condition |
| | C. | occasion | D. | pretext |

| 74. | A. | predominant | B. | meticulous |
| | C. | unyielding | D. | permissive |

| 75. | A. | waged | B. | admonished |
| | C. | hampered | D. | evoked |

| 76. | A. | contingent | B. | immeasurable |
| | C. | pathetic | D. | docile |

| 77. | A. | Pundits | B. | Connoisseurs |
| | C. | Advocates | D. | Culprits |

| 78. | A. | commended | B. | embroiled |
| | C. | divulged | D. | prosecuted |

| 79. | A. | Despite | B. | As a result of |
| | C. | Instead of | D. | Besides |

| 80. | A. | follows | B. | backfires |
| | C. | precedes | D. | succeeds |

IX. **Write a short essay in English of 150-200 words as your answer to the following question:**

Why is the United Nations following public opinion on climate change, and not leading public opinion about climate change?

マークシート記入例

東京の本会場でA級を受験する、国連 太郎さん、受験番号が「東京01-20001」、生年月日が「1980年10月24日」の場合の記入例です。

【受験番号/氏名】
それぞれ受験票の記載通りに記入してください。

受験番号	東京01-20001
氏　名	**国連 太郎**

【受験地区】
受験記号・番号の、都道府県部分を塗りつぶしてください。

【会場番号】
都道府県部分に続く2桁の数字を塗りつぶしてください。

【受験番号】
ハイフン（−）以降の5桁の数字を塗りつぶしてください。

【受験級】
「A」と記入し、下段のA級部分を塗りつぶしてください。

【生年月日】
4桁の西暦・月・日を塗りつぶしてください。
10未満の月・日の十の位は、「0」を塗りつぶしてください。

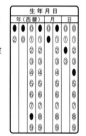

※HB以上の鉛筆を用いてマークをしてください。

※他の地区から会場を変更して受験する場合でも、受験票に記載されている受験地区・会場番号をマークしてください。

133

2020年
第2回試験

解答・解説

2020年　国連英検Ａ級第2回試験
解答・解説

＊〔　〕内は訳出上の補足や説明

| Ｉ | 『新 わかりやすい国連の活動と世界』に基づき，空所を埋めるのに最も適切なものを４つの選択肢の中から１つ選びなさい。 |

1.　解答：Ｂ

訳例　国連の本体は，総会，安全保障理事会，経済社会理事会，信託統治理事会，国際司法裁判所，事務局の６主要機関から構成される（『新 わかりやすい国連の活動と世界』p.42。以下，書名略）。

2.　解答：Ｄ

訳例　「国際連合」という名称は，フランクリン・Ｄ・ルーズベルト米大統領の発案による。正式に採用されたのは1942年，26カ国の代表が「ヒットラー主義打倒の闘い」において協力を誓い，連合国宣言に署名した時点であった（同 p.43）。

3.　解答：Ｃ

訳例　国連職員の話す言葉は，約170種類に及ぶ。言葉の混乱を避けるため，数カ国語が「公用語」あるいは「常用語」として指定されている（同 p.45）。

4.　解答：Ｃ

訳例　総会の定例会議は毎年９月の第３火曜日に始まり，12月半ばまで続く（同 p.54）。

5.　解答：Ａ

訳例　経済社会理事会は通常毎年１回，通常会期をニューヨークとジュネーブにおいて交互に開催していたが，現在は，人道支援部門を除き，毎年ニューヨークで開催している（同 p.57）。

6.　解答：Ｄ

訳例　人権理事会は総会で選出された47の加盟国代表から構成され，その構成は地

理的に公平な配分に基づく。理事国は，人権の促進と保護に関する貢献について誓約をする。選出された理事国は，人権の促進と保護において最高度の水準を保持するものとする（同 p.59）。

7. 解答：B

訳例　国際労働機関（ILO）は 1919 年，ヴェルサイユ条約の一部を成す形で，国際連盟と提携する自治機関として設立された（同 p.76）。

8. 解答：C

訳例　1960 年代以降，ユネスコの加盟国が増えると，新興独立国の支持を背景に，ユネスコが自立的な政策を展開するようになり，アメリカと対立を深めていった（同 p.78）。

9. 解答：D

訳例　1944 年のブレトンウッズ会議では，1930 年代に常態化したような為替管理や差別的関税を繰り返さないよう，大戦後の国際経済秩序を形成することが議論され，国際通貨基金協定が起草された（同 p.81）。

10. 解答：C

訳例　日本が国連の 80 番目の加盟国となった 1956 年は東西両陣営の緊張関係が緩和しつつあったいわゆる「雪どけ」の時代に当たる（同 p.165）。

Ⅱ 　下線を引いた動詞（句）の最も適切な変化形を 4 つの選択肢の中から 1 つ選びなさい。

11. 解答：D

解説　「同時性」を表す接続詞の as に注目する。主節の has ... lifted（現在完了形）は現在の状態を表す完了・結果用法。よって，現在形の D が正解。

12. 解答：D

解説　付帯状況を表す分詞構文と考えられる。よって，D が正解。

13. 解答：C

解説　leave O＋C に注目する。That は前文を指すので，そういうひどい干ばつが O＝C の状態を残した，と考える。よって，現在完了形の C が正解。

137

14. 解答：B

解説 ensure S＋V は現在進行中の対策の目的に相当する。よって，現在形の B が正解。

15. 解答：C

解説 bringing in grain を trucks の形容詞句と考える。よって，現在分詞の C が正解。

16. 解答：A

解説 seeking comment を messages and phone calls の形容詞句と考える。よって，現在分詞の A が正解。

17. 解答：D

解説 Government ... the nation で英文は完結しているので，guided by that assessment を分詞構文と捉え weighs ... and proceeds の並列構造にする。

18. 解答：A

解説 この with は付帯状況で，目的語と下線部動詞の関係は受け身になる。よって，過去分詞の A が正解。

19. 解答：A

解説 genetically modified corn は不定詞（形式主語）の意味上の主語なので，separated and sent と並列構造にすればよい。

20. 解答：B

解説 65 registered millers の形容詞句が続いている。よって，関係代名詞を使った B が正解。

訳例　南アフリカのジンバブエは，同国として最大の被害をもたらす恐れがある飢餓を回避する取り組みを始めるに当たり，遺伝子組み換えトウモロコシの輸入禁止措置を 12 年ぶりにひそかに解除した。
　　　南アフリカからの遺伝子組み換えトウモロコシ輸入が許可されるが，このト

ウモロコシは入念な検疫を受け，製粉されてジンバブエの主食であるコーンミールとなる。状況を知る3人の当局者が述べた。ただし，発表前であることからいずれも匿名を求めている。コーンミールは現地でサッザと呼ばれる主食の原料となるが，現在は国全体で不足している。

　ジンバブエは過去40年間で最悪の干ばつと闘っており，経済崩壊のただ中にある。このため人口の半分以上に当たる約800万人に食料支援が必要な状況だ。

　サハラ以南のアフリカでは南アフリカを除いては全体に遺伝子組み換えトウモロコシが嫌われており，ジンバブエでも国内の原種〔採種用の種〕に混じらないよう対策が施されている。上述の当局者の1人の話によると，穀物の輸入状況を監視するため，南アフリカに物流チームを派遣しているという。また，南アフリカとジンバブエの間に架かる橋で，アフリカ南部の国境の〔輸送路〕として最も交通量が多いベイトブリッジで遅れが出ないよう，穀物を輸入する輸送車向けに特別な税関を設ける計画も進められている。

　ペレンス・シリ農相と同省のジョン・バセラ常任秘書官は，コメントを求める問い合わせや電話に即座には答えなかった。ジンバブエ穀物製粉工業会のタファザ・ムサララ会長も問い合わせや電話には回答しなかった。

　政府のニック・マングワナ主席報道官は，「政府は遺伝子組み換えトウモロコシに関する立場について，国民の栄養上の必要とも勘案して評価しており，その結果に基づいて動いている」と述べたが，輸入禁止が解除されたかどうかは明言していない。

　ジンバブエのトウモロコシ収穫量は今季は〔前季比で〕50％以上の減少が予測され，80万～100万トンの供給不足となる公算が高い。

　主に食用として使用されている白トウモロコシの週間輸入量は，1月24日までの1週間で1万3,688トンと，ほぼ7年ぶりに過去最高を記録した。

　1月22日の製粉工業会の発表によると，南アフリカ産トウモロコシを毎月10万トン供給してもらう契約を結んだという。これまではトウモロコシが十分輸入されているという証拠はほとんどなかった。

　グレイン社のジャニー・ドゥ・ヴィイエCEOは，遺伝子組み換えトウモロコシを選別して直接処理〔工程〕へ送り込むことは可能で，ジンバブエはこれを過去にも実施したことがあるとしている。

　ヴィイエCEOは問い合わせに対して電子メールで次のように回答した。「歴史的に見てジンバブエは，遺伝子組み換えでないトウロモロコシだけを輸入しているが，それは食料安全の観点からではなく，原種の安全のためだ。戦略上，多国籍企業が供給する種に依存したくないと考えている」。

　商工省では昨年12月，手ごろな価格のコーンミールを供給すべく同省トウモロコシ補助金制度を導入したが，同制度には65の製粉業者が登録している。

139

<table>
<tr><td>Ⅲ</td><td>空所を埋めるのに文法的・論理的に最もふさわしいものを
4つの選択肢の中から1つ選びなさい。</td></tr>
</table>

21. 解答：D

解説 2つの不定詞に着目し，コロケーションの観点から boost ... measures と counter ... coronavirus epidemic を含む D を正解とする。

22. 解答：B

解説 接続詞 since に着目し，the outbreak と空所後の started で S+V が成立する B を正解に選ぶ。

23. 解答：A

解説 but のあとは S+V なので，B と D は簡単に除外できる。C は close to confirmed が文法的におかしい。

24. 解答：D

解説 prevent O from ... の語法が成立している D が正解。to＋空所で a "window of opportunity" を修飾する形容詞句になっている。

25. 解答：C

解説 関係代名詞 who に着目し，先行詞が人の A と C に絞る。A は目的語の位置にある place in systems が文法的におかしい。

26. 解答：A

解説 空所前の action と並列関係を築くには名詞で始める必要がある。これで C と D は除外できる。B は接続詞 while のあとの S+V が成立していない。

27. 解答：D

解説 if 節につながる主節が文法的に成立しているのは D のみ。

28. 解答：C

解説 factors の具体例が A, B, and C の構造で続いていることに着目する。

29. 解答：B

解説 空所前のコンマまでで文が完結し，あとに接続詞がないことから，分詞構文が続く。expressing ... and offering と並列関係が成立しているBが正解。

30. 解答：A

解説 provide support ... to China's に着目し，efforts のあとに形容詞句が続くAを選ぶ。

訳例　　新型コロナウィルスの感染拡大による死者が500人に迫る中，世界保健機関（WHO）の事務局長が水曜日，ウィルス流行を抑え込む国際的な措置を強化するため6億7,500万ドルの資金を援助するよう〔各国に〕呼びかけた。

テドロス・アダノム・ゲブレイェソス事務局長はジュネーブで発言し，最新のデータによると，12月31日に〔中国からWHOへ〕報告されたこの呼吸器系疾患（COVID-19）で，中国国内の感染者が2万4,363人，死者490人となったことを明らかにした。「流行開始以来，過去24時間で1日当たりの〔新規〕感染者数が最多（世界新規感染者3,925人）となった」。

テドロス氏はウィルスにより生じた懸念について触れながら，「武漢の人々が苦しい状況にあることを忘れてはいけない」と付言した。〔武漢は〕中国中央部で流行の中心となっている都市のことである。

同氏が報道陣に明らかにしたところによると，中国以外では24カ国で感染者191人，フィリピンで死者1人が報告されている。このうち31人は中国への渡航歴がないものの，いずれも感染確認者との接触者の近親者や，感染の発生地で流行の中心となっている武漢から来た人の近親者だという。

中国では〔世界〕感染者数の99%が発生しており，湖北省だけでそのうち80%を占める。このように中国国外で「感染者が比較的少ないこと」から，感染がグローバルな危機に発展するのを防ぐ「絶好のチャンス」が生まれていると，テドロス事務局長は力を込めた。

テドロス氏は，WHOの最大の懸念は感染検知能力を持たない国々へのウィルスの拡大だと強調するとともに，ウィルスのさらなる広がりを抑えるため，国際社会に対して連帯（政治的，技術的，経済的な連帯）を示すよう訴えた。

「私が最も心配しているのは，このウィルスが現れたとしても感染者を発見するシステムがない国々が現在あるということ。感染者を検査，診断，治療してこれ以上の人から人への伝染を防ぎ，医療従事者を守るため，脆弱な医療システムを強化すべく緊急の支援が必要だ」（同氏）。

「我々の強さは，我々の最弱リンク*以上には高まらない」と同氏は述べるとともに，感染拡大を抑えるべくWHOの緊急予備資金から900万ドルを拠出

したと付言した。これに加え，WHO ではマスク約 50 万枚と医療用手袋 35 万枚，呼吸器キット 4 万個，防護服約 1 万 8,000 着を 24 カ国へ配布した。

WHO ではさらに，ウィルス検査が速やかに行えるようにするため，検体 25 万個を世界 70 カ所以上の研究所に送った。「しかし必要な仕事はまだある」と同氏は述べた上で，戦略的準備および対応のために呼びかけた 6 億 7,500 万ドル〔の資金援助〕について，各国が自国民を保護する上で，よりよい予防措置やより速やかな診断によりどのように役立てられるのか，その概要を示した。

同氏は次のように述べた。「我々は人々が不安に駆られていることは理解している。それはもっともなことだが，いまは恐れているときではない。パニックに陥っているときではない。この流行を抑え込む絶好のチャンスが残っているうちに，理性的かつ証拠に基づいた対応と投資を行うときなのだ」。

WHO 健康危機対応統括者のマイケル・ライアン博士は報道陣に対し，コロナウィルスの治療効果が証明された薬はこれまでのところ存在しない，と述べた。同氏は，世界各国の疫学者で作る WHO の小チームが「中国の疫学者から学ぶため」中国入りする予定であることを確認するとともに，既往症がある高齢者が主に罹患（りかん）していると述べた。

（患者に対して）呼吸補助 / 支援を与えることは非常に重要だ」と同氏は付言し，「死者の中には多臓器不全が原因の人もいるが，重症患者も適時に十分な治療を受けられれば助かるだろう」と述べた。WHO では今回の流行について，中国で「非常に高い」リスクをもたらすとともに，地域的・世界的にもリスクが高いと考えている。

WHO のリスク評価は，今後のさらなる拡大の可能性や人間の健康に及ぼしうる影響，それに各国の準備態勢や対応措置の効力の違いなどの要素に基づくものだ。WHO は声明の中で，水曜日の呼びかけで要請した速やかな行動では，こうしたリスクや支援が必要な地域が対象となりうるとしている。

国連食糧農業機関 (FAO)，国際農業開発基金 (IFAD)，世界食糧計画 (WFP) は水曜日，中国の最高指導者に書簡を送り，感染流行と闘う中国に対して〔3者〕共同で連帯を表すとともに，支援を申し出た。

習近平国家主席宛てに連名の書簡を送ったもので，この中で 3 機関の長（屈冬玉 FAO 事務局長，ジルベール・ウングボ IFAD 総裁，デイヴィッド・ビーズリー WFP 事務局長）は中国国民の強靭さに敬意を示すとともに，緊急事態に対応する中国が行っている努力を称賛した。

いずれも本部をローマに置くこれら 3 機関は，今回の感染流行を「中国と世界の他の国々にとって医療の難しい課題」と述べるとともに，農村部を中心に国民に対するウィルスの影響を緩和しようとする中国の取り組みに対して，各機関の分野の専門知識を生かした支援を提供する用意があると約束した。

＊訳注：「最弱リンク理論」と呼ばれる考え方。

IV
以下の文章に最も適切に当てはまる語句のペアを
4つの選択肢の中から1つ選びなさい。

31. 解答：A

解説 第2空所の「スコットランドと北アイルランドを ＿＿＿＿ により失う」という文脈から A. secession が正解。第1空所はどの単語でも正解になりうる。

訳例 EU 離脱はイギリスにとって惨事だ。スコットランドと北アイルランドを分離独立により失うリスクを考えれば，大英帝国から「小イングランド」に戻る考えを受け入れたように見える。

32. 解答：D

解説 第1空所では A. dire と D. acute が候補になる。第2空所の「今後大きな食料危機は ＿＿＿＿」という文脈から，D. avert が正解。

訳例 東アフリカ地域はいま，気候ショックや紛争，重大な食料不安に加え，砂漠バッタによる飢餓の脅威にさらされている。国連の各救援機関の長が火曜日，共同で発言し，いま措置を講ずれば今後大きな食料危機は避けられると述べた。

33. 解答：B

解説 第1空所は原子力を動力源としているわけではないので A. powered を候補から外す。第2空所は北朝鮮の核保有が恒久化している状況を表す単語として，B. status quo を選びたい。D. era は a distinctive period of history なので，a new normal の意味では使えない。

訳例 北朝鮮の核搭載ミサイル兵器保有がますます永続化しそうな情勢となってきた。米政府は日本政府に対する配慮から，この現実を公式に承認することは今後も拒み続けるものとみられるが，地域は新しい状況が固定化してしまった。

34. 解答：C

解説 第1空所は concern に続く前置詞という観点から A. about と C. over が残る。第2空所は目的語の an information blackout に着目し C. amid を正解に選ぶ。

訳例 独立した国連の人権専門家らが火曜日，ミャンマー北西部で民間人の殺害や強制移動が発生しているとして重大な懸念を表明した。ラキン州とチン州の一部で情報統制が行われる中で，〔ミャンマー〕軍と〔少数民族〕武装勢力のアラカン軍との間の紛争が激化している〔ことによるもの〕。

35. 解答：C

解説 第1空所はC. secular を選ぶと，インドは宗教で国民を区別しないという文意に合致する。第2空所も C. on the basis of しか適さない。

訳例 インドは過去70年にわたり世俗国家にとどまる努力を重ねてきた。国民の大多数がヒンドゥー教徒でありながら，市民（市民と見なされる人々）をあえて宗教に基づいて区別しないことにしたのだ。

36. 解答：A

解説 第1空所はシリアの情勢を踏まえると A. stalled しか残らない。第2空所は put their weight にすると「重きを置く」で文意に合う。

訳例 シリアで和平と政治の両面が停滞していることから，国連のゲイル・ペデルセン〔シリア担当〕特使は水曜日，安全保障理事会の各国大使に対し，9年近くにもなる紛争を終わらせる解決策を見つけることに「重きを置く」よう呼びかけた。

37. 解答：B

解説 第1空所はU.S. troops を修飾するので B. stationed と C. deployed が残る。第2空所は Ankara がトルコを指すことを念頭に B. incursion を選ぶ。

訳例 前日夜行われた米国とトルコの大統領電話会談を受けて10月7日，シリア北部に駐留していた米軍部隊が撤退を開始した。〔その後〕48時間足らずの間にトルコは同地クルド人地域へ軍事侵攻を開始した。

38. 解答：D

解説 第1空所で絞り込むのは難しい。第2空所は inclusive society とすれば，with full respect for its multicultural nature ともイメージが重なる。

訳例 ミチェル・バチェレ国連人権高等弁務官は金曜日，南米のエクアドルにおける最近の〔政情〕不安による「大きな人的損失」を非難するとともに，エクアドル国内のすべての行為主体に対し，新たな紛争を防ぎ，「エクアドルの多文化性を十分に尊重した」包摂的な社会を築くために対話を行うよう呼びかけた。

39. 解答：B

解説 第1空所は A, B and C の並列関係に着目し，B. huddled と C.

collaborated を残す。第２空所はアメリカが置かれている状況を表しているので，C. detention では文意に合わない。

訳例 イラク国内に数万人の部隊を配置し，イラクの指導者と協議して法の制定を支援してきた米国。イラクが激しい抗議行動に見舞われる中で，この混乱から距離を置くようになった。

40. 解答：A

解説 第１空所は中国の補助金に対する一般常識を生かし A. distorting を選ぶ。D と組み合わせた market-manipulating という表現はない。第２空所の A. apparently は記事でよく見る表現。

訳例 日本，米国，欧州連合は火曜日，世界貿易機関のルールに基づき，市場をゆがめる〔産業〕補助金に対する禁止措置の拡大を提案した。中国を標的とする措置とみられる。

V

文法的，語法的にふさわしくないものを下線の中から１つ選びなさい。

41. 解答：B

解説 isolated → isolating。cultivating と並列構造なので -ing にしなければならない。

訳例 中国・武漢市で初めて報告された新型コロナウィルスについて，国立感染症研究所は金曜日，ウィルスを持つことが確認された日本在住者からの培養と分離に成功したと発表した。

42. 解答：A

解説 Once → As。森林火災が収束しない状況を説明しているので，once（いったん〜すると）では文意に合わない。

訳例 オーストラリアで「壊滅的」かつ甚大な森林火災の非常事態が続く中，国連の気候分野の専門家らは火曜日，火の動きが速く，火災に見舞われかねない状況にあることから，住民に引き続き厳重な警戒を求める政府の警告と同様の見解を述べた。

43. 解答：A

解説 keeping → to keep。manage の語法は manage to do（何とか〜する）。

訳例 苦労して築いた対中関係について，安倍晋三首相は新型コロナウィルス

COVID-19 の感染拡大によってその関係が損なわれるのをこれまで何とか防いできたが，〔いまは〕日本で新たな感染が確認されるたびにそれが難しくなってきている。

44.　解答：B

解説　of → as。her legacy ... an advocate for displaced persons に着目して適切な前置詞を選ぶ。

訳例　米国務省は水曜日，緒方貞子元国連難民高等弁務官の死去に対して追悼の意を表すとともに，同氏が避難民の擁護者として残した遺産は，世界中の人道的活動を行う人々を「鼓舞するもの」だと述べた。

45.　解答：D

解説　was carried → carried。carried out by the United States で直前の an airstrike を修飾している。

訳例　国連のアントニオ・グテーレス事務総長は，米国がイラクで行った空爆でイラン〔革命防衛隊〕の幹部司令官〔ガセム・ソレイマニ司令官〕が殺害されたことを受けて湾岸地域全体で緊張が高まっている現状に対し，深い懸念を示した。

46.　解答：A

解説　a global progress → global progress。progress は不可算名詞。a good education のように形容詞が付くと a がつく不可算名詞もあるが，progress は make good progress のように冠詞は不要。

訳例　貧困，飢餓，病気をなくす取り組みが世界的に進む一方，「新世代の格差」〔の存在〕は，多くの社会で機能不全が起きていることを示している——国連開発計画（UNDP）は月曜発表の最新報告書の中でこのように指摘している。

47.　解答：C

解説　accurate → accurately。translate を修飾するので副詞にしなくてはならない。

訳例　日本政府は，若手御曹司〔政治家〕の小泉進次郎環境相が先日，気候変動について述べた際，英語の「セクシー」という単語を使ったことについて，「正確な訳出は困難」とする正式の〔閣議〕決定を行った。同相の微妙な言葉遣いに対する公式訳の発表を避けた形だ。

48. 解答：D

解説 reached to → reached。reach a deal で「合意に達する」。

訳例 日本と韓国は，期限切れを迎える情報共有のための協定を継続させるべく金曜日にギリギリの合意に達したが，日曜日になって新たな非難合戦が勃発。米国の同盟国どうしとしての〔今後の〕関係改善に疑問符が付いた。

49. 解答：C

解説 would → will。「緊急対策を実施しない場合」というのは現実性があることなので仮定法は使えない。

訳例 国連ユネスコが金曜日に発表した新たなデータが明らかにしたところによると，緊急対策を実施しない場合，約1,200万人の子供が学校にまったく通えなくなり，中でも女子が「最も大きな障壁」にぶつかるという。

50. 解答：D

解説 is →トル。S (= the Secretary-General), V (= convened) はすでにあるので，この位置に be 動詞が入ることはない。

訳例 持続可能な開発目標達成のための投資の取り組み拡大を目指し，事務総長は水曜日，国連後援による新たな企業連合〔持続可能な開発のためのグローバル投資家（GISD）〕の初会合を招集した。持続可能性のための支出計画を議論する狙いで，支出額は数兆ドル規模となる可能性が高い。

VI 以下の文章の中に含まれる太字の語句および空所の意味として文脈上最も近いものを4つの選択肢の中から1つ選びなさい。

51. 解答：B

解説 空所前後の意味は「母が低額で医療を受けられるようにするには父が ＿＿＿＿ことが必要となった」なので，come out of retirement（引退を撤回する）が適切。

52. 解答：D

解説 make a move は take action と同じ意味をもつ。

53. 解答：C

解説 空所前後の意味は「私が目を向けるべき何か別の ＿＿＿＿ があるに違いない」。その前に，政権が民主党に移っても問題は解決されなかった，と

あるので C.「阻害要因」が正解。

54. 解答：B

解説 直前の that は if 節を指す。それが them（= people）を spur する，という文脈なので同義語である B.「駆り立てる」が正解。

55. 解答：B

解説 It should have been a great moment とあるが，空所後に「国は政府の役割をめぐる激烈な論争へと突入していった」とある。よって，In place of the great moment と同義の Instead が正解。

56. 解答：A

解説 「事実に ＿＿＿ するために最大限の努力をした」という文脈なので, stick to ... の意味は adhere to ...。よって，それと同義 abide by を選ぶ。

57. 解答：A

解説 「政府運営の制度に手を出すなという要求を〔当の〕政府に対して行う」という行為を著者は皮肉な事態と捉えている。sarcasm は人を小馬鹿にするニュアンスがあり，この文脈には適さない。

58. 解答：C

解説 文脈から，著者が that 節の現実に対して疑問を呈していることは明らか。よって，C.「いかにして」が正解。

59. 解答：B

解説 この文脈で warped ＞ warp は influence someone in a way that has a harmful effect という意味。

60. 解答：C

解説 「多数の人が自分の考えを確認するためだけに情報を求め，政府が出すデータや政府に関するデータを市場に ＿＿＿＿」という文脈なので，C. flooding が正解。

訳例　　　私は何とか結果を出そうとそれまで 10 年をワシントン D.C. で過ごしてきた。私が政治に召命されていることは聖職者の召命と同じようなもので，私は政治をやる運命なのだと言ってくれる人はたくさんいた。事の起こりは 2000 年，一本の電話がかかってきたことからだった。しかしそれは神からではなく，ワシントン D.C. からでもなかった。母からの電話であった。医者の検査で胸にしこりが見つかり，乳がんと診断されたというのである。父がすでに退職していたため母はメディケアの給付対象外となっており，母が低額で医療を受けられるようにするには父が再就職することが必要となった。

　　元気な二十歳そこそこの青年であった私は何とかしなければと思った。数年が過ぎ，イラクでの戦争が終わったころ，私はヴァーモント州のバーリントンへ車で向かっていた。ハワード・ディーン州知事の下で働くためである。私はそれまで投票したことがなかったが，ディーンは医師であり，医療の面では本拠地のヴァーモント州で理に適った措置を講じていた。大統領選への立候補者の中で唯一，母の医療保険料を引き下げることができ，父が再び退職できるようにしてくれそうな人であった。私の政治家としてのキャリアはこうして始まった。しかし，私は自分が解決しようと乗り出した問題を解決に向けて進められていないことが明らかになった。2006 年の下院選では民主党に過半数を与えたのに医療については依然として何の動きもないのを見て，私は民主党を選挙で選んで問題を解決させるやり方は，あまり役に立たないと悟った。私が目を向けるべき何か別の阻害要因があるに違いない〔と考えたのだ〕。

　　私はサンライト・ファウンデーションに新しい仕事を得て，技術者のチームを指揮する立場にあった。チームの使命は，政府のデータを自由化して分析すること，国民が選挙についてもっと情報を得た上で〔投票の〕判断をしやすくすることであった。米国民に対して米議会が買収されつつあるという厳然たる事実を示すことができれば，行動につなげることができるはずだ。サンライトに勤めて 2 年が経ったころ——母が宣告されてからはまる 8 年が過ぎていた——私はバラク・オバマ新大統領が医療の問題を持ち出すのを注視していた。それは，喜ばしい時となるはずであった。十年来の私の希望がかなうのだから。しかし逆に，私が見守る中で国は政府の役割をめぐる激烈な論争へと突入していった。

　　メディアはありとあらゆるグラフや表で埋め尽くされた。米国人の医療費や〔医療機関での〕待ち時間，政府の効率性，カナダはどうやっているのか，高齢者は医療をどうしているのか，何らかの医療改革法案を通過させた場合に米国人にはどんな薬が使えるようになり，どんな薬が使えなくなるのかなど。サンライト社〔の仕事〕で，私たちは事実に忠実であろうと最大限の努力をした。一般の人が医療関連の討論をオンラインで視聴できる「サンライトライブ」を作ったし，米議会議員が話をするときは，全員〔の映像〕について，その横に医療関連業界から受けた献金の額が表示されるようにした。

その長い激烈な議論が行われていたころ，私は散歩でホワイトハウスへ行ってみた。あのプラカード，あの不快な7つの単語を見たのはそのときだった。「政府は私のメディケアに手を出すな」——そう抗議する人に私は話しかけ，プラカードについて尋ねた。その男性はむしろよい教育を受けた人のようであった——もちろん怒ってはいるが，馬鹿ではなかった。この男性は情報が足りないわけではないのに，自分が頭上に掲げたプラカードが，政府運営の制度に手を出すなという要求を〔当の〕政府に対して行うという皮肉になっていることには思いいたってはいなかった。ご本人としては，至極当然のことなのだ。教育ある頭のよい人たちがゆがめられた現実をなぜか信じることができるようになるのだが，それは一体どうしてなのだろうか？

その瞬間，ある考えが頭に浮かんだ。人が生まれつき持つ，あるいは学習して得た，適切に情報を処理する能力が，精神のメカニズムにごみくずを投入することでゆがめられるとしたら？

人間〔の体〕が食べ物から作られることを私たちは知っている。〔ならば〕人間は自分が閲覧する情報によっても作られるはずではないか？　不健康な食事によって食品依存症になるように，不健全な情報閲覧によって悪い情報利用習慣が身についてしまうなら，透明性など何の役に立つだろう？　私はサンライト・ファウンデーションを辞めた。私が探し求めていた答えは透明性ではなかったのだ。多数の人が自分の考えを確認するためだけに情報を求めるなら，政府が出すデータや政府に関するデータを市場に溢れさせても，理論家が予言するほどの効果は得られないだろう。データは左翼と右翼の集票組織によってゆがめられ，アメリカを動かし続けるごみくずが増えるだけになってしまうのだ。

| **VII** | 下線部の単語や句の意味を最もよく表しているものを
4つの選択肢の中から1つ選びなさい。 |

61.　解答：A

 critical はこの場合 serious, uncertain, and possibly dangerous の意。よって最も近いのは A.「差し迫った」。

62.　解答：C

 原形の mitigate は make something less harmful, serious の意。よって最も近いのは C.「和らげる」。

63.　解答：B

 propel はこの場合 drive something in a particular direction の意。よ

150

って最も近いのは B. 「推進する」。

64. 解答：D
解説 acceleration はこの場合 increase in speed の意。よって最も近いのは D. 「促進」。

65. 解答：C
解説 reframe は frame a concept differently の意。よって最も近いのは C. 「再評価する」。

66. 解答：D
解説 symbiotic は involving things in a way that they depend on each other の意。よって最も近いのは D. 「相互の」。

67. 解答：C
解説 原形の emulate はこの場合 try to do something as well as someone else because you admire them の意。よって最も近いのは C. 「複製する」。

68. 解答：A
解説 transition はこの場合 the process of changing from one state to another の意。よって最も近いのは A. 「進化」。

69. 解答：B
解説 cusp はこの場合 a point of transition between two different states の意。よって最も近いのは B. 「境界」。

70. 解答：D
解説 alleviate はこの場合 make a problem less severe の意。よって最も近いのは D. 「抑える」。

訳例　ポルトガルで数カ月後に開催される第2回〔国連〕海洋会議は，水生生物と陸上生物の健全性を確保する上で「決定的な瞬間」となるはずだ——準備が進

151

む中，〔ティジャニ・ムハンマド゠バンデ〕国連総会議長が火曜日，このように述べた。

「水生生物は陸上生物にとっても不可欠なものだ」と同議長はいう。海は「我々が吸い込む酸素の半分」を産出するほか，世界中の何百万もの人に食料を与えており，「巨大な吸熱源，炭素吸収源」として気候変動を緩和する上で根本的に重要な役割を果たしている。

6月2日から6日までリスボンで開かれる今回の海洋会議の目的は，科学に基づく革新的な解決策をグローバルな海洋に関する取り組みの形で推進することだ。世界の海洋関連経済〔の生産額〕は年間約1.5兆ドルとみられている。水産養殖は食料部門の中でも最も成長率が高い部門であり，漁業関連の雇用は全世界で3億5,000万人に達している。

同議長は次のように述べた。「海洋環境が健全であることは，持続可能な開発アジェンダ全体を達成する上で，計り知れない可能性を秘めている。しかし，海洋資源の持続不可能な利用（つまり乱用）や気候変動，汚染はいずれも，海が持つ我々を養う力に対して脅威となっている」。

今年は「行動と遂行の10年」の最初の年となっており，持続可能な開発目標（SDGs）の目標の中で今年達成すべきものについては〔その取り組み〕を加速することが必要だ。うち3分の2は，環境の健全性に関係する。

議長は次のように説明した。「SDG 14＝海の豊かさを守ろう〔日本語公式訳〕に関連するいくつかの目標を達成しなければならない。自然に対する我々の理解を，2030アジェンダ実行を加速するものとして位置づけ直すためだ」。

「水生生物と陸上生物は共生関係にある」と議長は述べるとともに，「汚染によって海が持つ人間の命を養う力が阻害されている」と指摘した。議長は，昨年の国連環境総会で出された，2030年までに使い捨てプラスチック製品を削減することを求める閣僚宣言について，「よりよい世界を築く多国間の取り組み」を示すものだと述べるとともに，この指導力を海洋会議でも見習って「同宣言が水生生物〔の環境を〕変えるような影響力を持つようにすること」が重要だと強調した。

サンゴ礁には海の生物の4分の1が生息しているが，これまでに半分が失われ，世界の食料安全保障にマイナスの影響を及ぼしている。また，報告や管理がなされていない違法な漁業が生態系にいっそう負担をかけている。さらに，気候変動が引き起こす海水面の上昇によって，小島嶼開発途上国を筆頭に，存続にかかわる脅威にさらされている。

「我々はこの国々を連帯し，支援しなければならない。これは我々すべてのためだ」。総会議長はこのように述べるとともに，海洋の健全性を改善することが「我々の未来を守るカギになる」と強調した。

議長は，グリーン経済への移行が「我々の海と世界を守る上で不可欠」と述べるとともに，来年から「持続可能な開発のための海洋科学の10年」が始ま

ることを改めて指摘した。

　国連海洋特使で，国連総会議長を務めたこともあるピーター・トムソン氏は，海洋をめぐる5つの大きな問題について概要を述べた。汚染（プラスチック，工業的農業の汚水など）と有害行為による漁業の持続可能性〔毀損〕はいずれも「2030年までに顕著に修復することが可能である」。これに対して，修復がより困難な問題は，酸性化や脱酸素化，海洋の温度上昇に関係するもので，いずれも温室効果ガスの排出とつながりがある。

　特使は「これら3つに関しては修復期間が〔他より〕はるかに長くなる状況だ」と述べるとともに，「明日にも適切な対応をしたとしても」数百年かかるだろうが，それでも「危機を脱する作業が始められるように」〔明日にも適切な対応を〕始めなければならないと指摘した。

　また，全員に「良い意味での転換点」に注目するよう促し，そうした転換点は「皆さんが思っているより近いところにある」と力を込めるとともに，さらにこうした転換点として，「科学と革新の増強」や，「このリスボン会議で集中的に議論する」その他の解決策などが含まれると述べた。特使は，途上国が持続可能な農業や風力発電所，海運業のグリーン化に関わろうとする「強い意志」について触れ，「我々はいま，大きな，良い方向への革命のとば口に立っている」と述べた。

　アントニオ・グテーレス国連事務総長はニューヨークで記者会見に臨み，進行する気候危機にとっての海洋の重要性や，気候危機を緩和する解決策について述べた。事務総長の説明によると，「海洋の温度が上がると氷が融け，氷床が太陽光を反射する重要な機能が失われ，それによって海洋の温度上昇がさらに進む」という。そして，氷が融けて海の温度が上がると，海面が上昇すると同時に，蒸発する水の量が増えるため，「ますます降水量が増えて，沿岸部の都市やデルタ地帯にとって脅威となる」。

　事務総長は，昨年は海水温度と平均海水位が「記録が残る中で最高」となったと指摘し，科学者らが現在主張している内容を明らかにした。「現在の海水温は広島型原爆が1秒に5個落とされたのと同じペースで上昇している」という。

VIII 文脈上，空所を埋めるのに最もふさわしいものを
4つの選択肢の中から1つ選びなさい。

71.　解答：D

解説 空所前後の意味は，「この裁判は数週間後に判決が下されるや，コロンビアの中絶法を ＿＿＿＿＿ する可能性がある」。よって，D.「変える」が正解。

72. 解答：B

解説 elective abortion で人工中絶の意味。本文中でも abortion だけで人工中絶の意味を表しているが，ここは各国の法律の違いを述べる箇所なので正確な語が使われているとみられる。よって，B.「選択できる」が正解。

73. 解答：A

解説 「同氏は3つの例外規定が憲法違反だと主張している」のあとに「中絶手術はすべて『母体と胎児の両方にとって』健康上のリスクをもたらす」とその根拠が書かれている。on the grounds that ... で「～を根拠として」という意味。

74. 解答：D

解説 空所前後の意味は，「中絶反対派は，2006年以降コロンビア当局が手続きに対してあまりに _____ になった」。よって，D.「寛大な」が正解。

75. 解答：A

解説 The woman's ex-boyfriend ... a widely reported campaign に着目し，適切な動詞を選ぶ。wage a campaign で「キャンペーンを行う」の意。

76. 解答：B

解説 空所前後の意味は，「例外規定はコロンビア国民に _____ 害を及ぼす」。よって，B.「計り知れない」が正解。

77. 解答：C

解説 ... argue that のあとに，中絶の全面的な合法化がもたらす利点が述べられている。よって，C.「賛成派」が正解。

78. 解答：D

解説 空所前後の意味は，「中絶の容疑で _____ された女性は2,290人」。ここは，中絶の合法化を主張する側が出したデータなので，D.「訴追された」が正解。

79. 解答：A

解説 「近年，この地域全体にわたって抗議の波が起きている」に続き，「ラテンアメリカで中絶を合法化した国は2012年のウルグアイ以降は例がない」とあるので，A.「〜にも関わらず」が正解。

80. 解答：B

解説 空所前の意味は，「特にベルナル氏の自由化に逆行する試みが_____した場合には，コロンビアで出される判決は潮目を変える」。よって，B.「裏目に出る」が正解。

訳例　　反人工妊娠中絶の活動家，ナタリア・ベルナル・カーノがコロンビアの最高裁判所に起こした訴訟。この裁判は数週間後に判決が下されるや，コロンビアの中絶法に変革をもたらす可能性がある——ただし，同氏が望むような仕方で〔変革を引き起こすこと〕はおそらくない。

　　コロンビアでは強力な権限を持つ憲法裁判所の2006年判決以来，女性にはレイプあるいは近親相姦の場合や，胎児に致死的な異常がある場合，あるいは母親の心身の健康に危険を及ぼす場合に妊娠中絶が認められてきた。

　　これらの3つの例外によってコロンビアは，中絶に対して他に見られない厳しい姿勢を取るラテンアメリカとカリブ諸国の中では中道派となっている。この地域ではエルサルバドルとドミニカ共和国を含む6カ国が，事由にかかわらず中絶を全面的に禁止。ウルグアイとキューバ，ガイアナだけが妊娠初期の人工中絶を認めている。

　　弁護士のベルナル氏は昨年，憲法裁判所に2件の訴訟を起こした。コロンビアを前者の陣営に戻そうとの願いからだ。同氏は3つの例外規定が憲法違反だと主張しているが，その根拠は，中絶手術はすべて「母体と胎児の両方にとって」健康上のリスクをもたらすからだ〔という〕。

　　だが，この訴訟を審理する9人の判事の1人，アレハンドロ・リナレス・カンティージョ判事は，そもそも裁判所は中絶がなぜ違法なのかを考えるべきだと主張している。同判事は2月19日，他の判事に対し，妊娠16週以内の中絶について全面合法化を検討するよう求める正式な提案書を提出した。

　　リナレスとベルナルの両氏は，カトリックが国民の4分の3近くを占めるコロンビアに熾烈な論争を再び巻き起こした。3月初めにも下されるとみられる判決は，コロンビア国内はもちろん他のラテンアメリカ諸国でも大きく注目されるだろう。

　　中絶反対派は，2006年以降コロンビア当局が手続きについて寛容になりすぎたと言っている。〔事実〕保守的な政治家らは，西部の都市ポパヤンの女性

が，精神健康上の問題から1月に妊娠7カ月で合法中絶をしたケースに対して激しい憤りを表明した。

　女性の元交際相手は中絶を望んでいなかった。そして，女性が中絶を決めたことに対して運動を始め，抗議活動をしたり，後には提訴すると脅したりして，これが広く報道された。

　ベルナル氏は，ポパヤンの女性が使ったような例外規定は「コロンビア国民に計り知れない害を及ぼす」と主張する。〔引用部分は〕コロンビアの「エル・エスペクタドル」紙に話したもので，〔害の例として〕中絶を行った女性の「心的外傷後ストレス」や「重い抑うつ症状」などを挙げている。

　ベルナル氏は，リベラルな傾向で知られるリナレス判事は偏向しているとして，この件に関与しないよう要請を何度か行ったが認められなかった。

　中絶権擁護派の各団体は，ポパヤンの事例は合法中絶を受けることさえ難しい現状を示す例だとしている。家族計画〔を指導する〕NPOのプロファミリアによると，この女性は妊娠3カ月になる前から〔すでに〕中絶を希望していたが，衛生当局に断られたという。同NPOでは，中絶を望む女性は94%が妊娠15週以内に中絶していると述べている。

　人権擁護派の弁護士で，ニューヨークの女性平等センターでラテンアメリカ部長を務めるパウラ・アビラ・ギレン氏は，現行法は「公的医療制度を利用しているより貧しい女性」を差別するものだと話す。公的医療制度においては3つの例外を認める法律がつぎはぎ的に実施されているが，裕福な女性は民間の医師の手による中絶をより容易に受けることができるというのだ。

　賛成派は，コロンビアで中絶を全面的に合法化すれば，女性が医療支援を必要とする場合にお役所手続きの遅れもなくなるし，逮捕や訴追のおそれからも解放されると主張する。コロンビアの司法長官が昨年発表したデータによると，2005年から2017年までの間に中絶の容疑で訴追を受けた女性は2,290人（未成年者502人を含む）となっている。

　現地報道によれば，裁判所が2006年の判決を覆す可能性は低いという。すでに何度かにわたって3つの例外が合憲であるとの判断を示しているからだ。

　ただ，最長で妊娠16週までの中絶を合法化すべきというリナレス氏の提案に関する結果がどうなるかは，それほどはっきりしていない。日刊新聞エル・ティエンポ紙によれば，リナレス氏を含む判事9人のうち4人は賛成，3人は反対する可能性が高い。浮動票となる可能性が非常に高い残り2人は，ギレン氏によればいずれも女性だという。

　近年，この地域全体にわたって抗議の波が起きているが，ラテンアメリカで中絶を合法化した国は2012年のウルグアイ以降は例がない。アルゼンチンの活動家らが合法化法案の可決を目指した試みは2018年に失敗に終わった。下院は可決したが上院が僅差で否決したのだ。中絶を支持するアルゼンチンの議員らは，アルベルト・フェルナンデス新大統領が任期中の中絶合法化を公約し

156

たことから，まもなく再び行動を始めるものとみられている。

　ギレン氏は，これまでの 3 年間はこの地域の中絶権〔をめぐる状況〕の転機だったように感じられると言う。「ちょっと休んだあと，力を取り戻してまた前に進みはじめた感じだ」。コロンビアで出される判決は潮目を変えることになるかもしれない。特にベルナル氏の自由化に逆行する試みが裏目に出た場合には〔その可能性が高くなる〕と同氏は言う。「地域全体で中絶の議論が行われている中，そうなれば非常によい先例となるだろう」。

IX

以下の質問に対し，150 〜 200 語の短いエッセイを英語で書きなさい。

質問文：「気候変動に関して国連が世論の後を追い，世論をリードしていないのはなぜか？」

解答例　　The UN follows rather than leads public opinion about climate change for three reasons: to act as fact giver rather than lobby group; to support diverse ways people focus on climate issues; and by serving as a public opinion forum.

　First, the UN role as fact giver is rooted in its specialized agencies. For example, the World Meteorological Organization (WMO), ratified in 1950 with 140 years of scientific research, reportage, and action planning since its formation, provides precise weather trend information. WMO, UNEP, IPCC, UNFCCC, and COP activities all increase public knowledge.

　Second, SDG 13 Climate Action—education to raise awareness of adaptation and impact; focusing on youth, women, local and marginalized community involvement; and providing funding to developing countries—supports diverse ways everyday people turn their opinions into actions.

　Third, the UN's traditional role is to serve as a forum for world public opinion. NGOs and advocacy groups, like Greenpeace and Greta Thunberg's *FridaysForFuture* activist movement, mobilize thousands of people worldwide at events like the UN September 2019 New York Climate Action Summit.

　In conclusion, the UN—as fact provider, through SDGs, and as

2020年
第2回
解答・解説

157

a world forum—supports public opinion's demands for immediate action to deal with climate change.

解説　全体を通して，国連システムに関する正確な知識を織り交ぜつつ，意見や論評を述べるようにするとよい。

第1パラグラフでは主題を提示し，その理由を簡潔に3つ列挙している。

第2パラグラフでは，世界気象機関（WMO）を代表的な例として，事実を周知する国連の役割について述べている。

第3パラグラフでは，SDGs の目標13「気候変動に具体的な対策を」を例に人々が行動できるさまざまな方法を国連が支援していることを示している。

第4パラグラフでは，ニューヨーク気候行動サミットといった大規模なイベントを通じて，国連が世論形成の場になっていると指摘している。

第5パラグラフでは，3つの論拠を振り返りつつ，国連は気候変動に対する世論の要求を支持している，と結んでいる。

訳例　気候変動に関して国連が世論をリードするよりむしろ世論の後を追っているのは，次の3つの理由からである。すなわち，圧力団体としてよりも，むしろ事実を周知する者として行動するため，気候問題に取り組むさまざまな方法を支援するためであり，また，世論形成の場としての役割を果たすことによってである。

第一に，事実を周知するという国連の役割は，専門機関の中に定着している。たとえば，世界気象機関（WMO）（1950年〔専門機関として〕承認，発足以来140年にわたり科学研究，報告，行動計画策定を行っている）は，正確な気象動向情報を提供している。WMO, UNEP, IPCC, UNFCCC, COP の活動はいずれも一般の人々の知識を高めるものである。

第二に，SDGs 目標13「気候変動に具体的な対策を」（適応および影響に対する意識を高める教育，青年，女性，地域コミュニティーおよび社会的に疎外されたコミュニティーの参画重視，途上国への資金提供）は，一般の人々が自分の考えを行動に移す多様なやり方を支援するものである。

第三に，国連の従来からの役割は，世界の世論形成の場となることである。グリーンピースやグレタ・トゥンベリの活動家運動「フライデーズ・フォー・フューチャー」のような NGO や権利擁護団体は，国連が2019年9月に開催したニューヨーク気候行動サミットなどのイベントに世界中から数千人を動員している。

結論としては，国連は SDGs を通じて事実を周知するものとして，また，世界の世論形成の場として，気候変動に対処する早急な行動に対する世論の要求を支持している。

I
1. B　2. D　3. C　4. C　5. A　6. D　7. B　8. C　9. D　10. C

II
11. D　12. D　13. C　14. B　15. C　16. A　17. D　18. A　19. A　20. B

III
21. D　22. B　23. A　24. D　25. C　26. A　27. D　28. C　29. B　30. A

IV
31. A　32. D　33. B　34. C　35. C　36. A　37. B　38. D　39. B　40. A

V
41. B　42. A　43. A　44. B　45. D　46. A　47. C　48. D　49. C　50. D

VI
51. B　52. D　53. C　54. B　55. B　56. A　57. A　58. C　59. B　60. C

VII
61. A　62. C　63. B　64. D　65. C　66. D　67. C　68. A　69. B　70. D

VIII
71. D　72. B　73. A　74. D　75. A　76. B　77. C　78. D　79. A　80. B

2次試験（面接テスト）について

　2次試験は，特A級およびA級の1次試験合格者を対象に，第1回目は7月中旬の日曜日，第2回目は12月中旬の日曜日に実施されます。

　特A級は外国人面接官1名，日本人面接官1名との2対1でのインタビュー，A級は外国人面接官と1対1でのインタビューです。面接時間は，特A級が15分，A級が10分です。A級については会場によりSkype等によるオンライン面接となる場合もあります。また面接テストの内容は公正な評価を行うため，すべて録音（オンライン面接の場合は録画）され，一定期間試験記録として保管されます。

　外国人面接官は，インタビュアーとしての研修を受け，最終審査に合格した英語のネイティブスピーカーです。外国人面接官の選抜には，国籍や人種のバランスも考慮されています。日本人面接官は，外務省大使OBなど外交実務経験者，または大学教授です。大使経験者は英語を駆使し，なおかつ世界で活躍した人々であり，大学教授はTOEIC® 満点，国連英検特A級合格，通訳案内業国家試験合格など，公的に英語力を証明できる資格を持ち，なおかつ国際舞台で活躍している人々です。

　2次試験では，まず面接シート（INTERVIEW SHEET）に事前に必要事項を英語で書き，入室と同時に面接シートを面接官に渡します。受験者が記入したくないと思う事項については書く必要はありません。面接シートは次ページのとおりです。面接シートの目的の1つは，受験者にとって身近な話題からインタビューを始め，リラックスした雰囲気で試験を行うことですから，面接の話題にしてほしいような内容はぜひ記入しておきましょう。受験者が着席すると面接が始まります。国連英検の面接官はインタビュアーとしての訓練を受けた専門家ですから，受験者が落ち着いて面接を受けられるように配慮しています。多くの場合，受験者にとって話のしやすい身近な話題から会話が始まり，質問は徐々に国際事情へと発展します。特定のトピックについて数分間のスピーチをするといったことはないため，自分にとって興味があり，得意とする分野に話題を導くことができ

れば有利となるでしょう。ただ，面接官は国際事情に詳しいので，日頃から
英字新聞をよく読み，幅広い知識を身につけておくことが必要不可欠です。

面接シート
INTERVIEW SHEET

受験級 Class	受験記号・番号	Name	
		氏名	

【記入上の注意 Notes】
1．下記の各項目を英語で記入して下さい。ただし、答えたくない項目は記入しなくて構いません。
2．記入された内容や記入量によって、試験の採点が影響されることはありません。

a. Family 家族（例：Father,Mother,Two brothers,One Daughter）

b. Home Address 現住所（区、市、郡まで。例：Nerima-ku,Tokyo）

c. Occupation 職業（例：Student,Office worker,Housewife,Bank clerk）

d. Special Qualifications 特技（例：Computer）

e. Education 教育（専攻のみ。例：Western History,Economics）

f. Hobbies,Interests,Special Concerns 趣味・興味を持っていること（例：Tennis,World Peace）

g. Your Favorite Authors 好きな作家・愛読書（例：Dickens,B.Russell）

h. Persons You Respect 尊敬する人物（例：My Father,Lincoln）

i. Foreign Countries Visited 海外経験（なければ None,あれば場所、時期、期間、目的）

j. Foreign Countries You Want to Visit 訪れたい国（例：India,Ireland）

国連英検の面接では，ただ単に国際事情の知識があるだけでは不十分です。日本人として，日本が国際社会でどのように行動したらよいか，どのようにすれば国際貢献できるのかといった視点から，理路整然かつ論理的に話ができる必要があります。付け焼刃の国際事情の知識ではとても太刀打ちできません。広く浅く議論を無難にこなせる分野だけではなく，深い議論が可能な分野もいくつか持っていることが必要です。

　面接において，日本との関係が希薄な国際事情について詳しく問われることはあまりありません。たとえ面接官が外交実務経験の豊富な大使経験者であっても，世界中の国際会議などで講演を常に行っている大学教授であっても，あくまで日本と日本人という視点からの質問が中心となります。

　２次試験の評価方法は，以下の４分野（合計７項目，括弧内は配点の割合）についてそれぞれ 10 段階で採点され，配点の割合に準じた得点の総合点＝総合評価で合否が判定されます。

　特 A 級は総合評価で 8 点以上，A 級は 7 点以上が合格です。

Examiner's analysis of candidate's strengths and weaknesses (Circle on number between 1 and 10 for each area of ability, adding "+" if desired.)					
Level of Strength / Area of Ability	Weak	Middle Range	Strong	Weight	Office Use
1) Comprehension	1　2　3	4　5　6　7	8　9　10	25.00%	
2) Speaking: Pronunciation	1　2　3	4　5　6　7	8　9　10	25.00% (6.25%)	
Fluency	1　2　3	4　5　6　7	8　9　10	(6.25%)	
Structure	1　2　3	4　5　6　7	8　9　10	(6.25%)	
Vocabulary	1　2　3	4　5　6　7	8　9　10	(6.25%)	
3) Communication	1　2　3	4　5　6　7	8　9　10	25.00%	
4) Knowledge (International Affairs)	1　2　3	4　5　6　7	8　9　10	25.00%	

　なお，特 A 級・A 級で実施される２次試験（面接テスト）の様子を紹介した動画が国連英検のホームページ上で公開されています。

　http://www.kokureneiken.jp/about/interviewmodel

国連英検実施要項

主　　　催 問い合わせ先	公益財団法人 日本国際連合協会 国連英検事務局 〒104-0031　東京都中央区京橋 3-12-4 MAOビル 4 階 TEL 03-6228-6831 ／ FAX 03-6228-6832 http://www.kokureneiken.jp/

※最新の情報は国連英検ホームページ http://www.kokureneiken.jp/ で確認すること。

試験日		1 次試験	2 次試験
	第 1 回	毎年 5 月下旬の日曜日	毎年 7 月中旬の日曜日
	第 2 回	毎年 10 月下旬の日曜日	毎年 12 月中旬の日曜日

※ 2 次試験は特 A 級・A 級のみ。

試験地	■ 1 次試験…札幌・仙台・長野・さいたま・千葉・東京・神奈川・ 　　　　　名古屋・金沢・神戸・京都・大阪・広島・福岡・鹿児 　　　　　島・那覇の予定 ■ 2 次試験…特 A 級：東京・大阪 　　　　　※特 A 級・A 級の併願者の 2 次試験はすべて東京・大阪で行なわれる。 　　　　　A 級：札幌・仙台・東京・名古屋・大阪・福岡・鹿児 　　　　　　　　島・那覇の予定 受験会場名，所在地は受験票に明示される。受験地の変更はできない。なお， 1 次試験を特別会場で受験した受験者の 2 次試験は，最寄りの試験会場となる。 ※ただし，会場は毎回変更の可能性がある。
検定料 （税込）	特 A 級…12,500 円　　　A 級…10,000 円　　　B 級…7,500 円 C 級…4,500 円　　　　D 級…4,000 円　　　E 級…3,000 円 ※一度納入された検定料は返却できない。申し込み後の変更もできない。 ※事務局が申込書を検定料の受領後，受付完了。
併願受験 検定料 （税込）	特 A 級＋ A 級＝ 20,000 円　　　　A 級＋ B 級＝ 15,000 円 B 級＋ C 級＝ 11,000 円　　　　C 級＋ D 級＝ 8,000 円 D 級＋ E 級＝ 6,000 円 ※一度納入された検定料は返却できない。申し込み後の変更もできない。 ※事務局が申込書を検定料の受領後，受付完了。
1 次試験の 開始時間	A 級　C 級　E 級……午前 10 時 30 分（集合時間午前 10 時） 特 A 級　B 級　D 級……午後 2 時（集合時間午後 1 時 30 分）

試験方法	■ 1 次試験		

<table>
<tr><td rowspan="11">試験方法</td><td colspan="3">■ 1 次試験</td></tr>
<tr><td>級</td><td>試験方法</td><td>試験時間</td></tr>
<tr><td>特 A・A</td><td>筆記試験のみ</td><td>120 分</td></tr>
<tr><td>B</td><td rowspan="4">リスニングテスト
筆記試験</td><td>120 分</td></tr>
<tr><td>C・D</td><td>100 分</td></tr>
<tr><td>E</td><td>80 分</td></tr>
</table>

■ 2 次試験

※特 A 級・A 級の 1 次試験合格者および 1 次試験免除者が対象。

※面接シートに事前に所要事項を英語で書き込み，外国人面接官などの質問事項に答える。

※ A 級については会場により Skype 等によるオンライン面接になる場合もある。

※面接の内容は試験実施の品質向上と厳正さを担保することを目的に録音（オンラインの場合は録画）される。

合格発表

合格者には合格カードを発行

試験結果は郵送にて通知。

	1 次試験	2 次試験
第 1 回	毎年 6 月下旬	毎年 8 月中旬
第 2 回	毎年 11 月下旬	毎年 1 月中旬

受験申し込み要項

●併願の場合

午前午後で隣接する 2 つの級を同日に受験することができる。併願を希望する場合は「受験申込書」の併願欄に記入して申し込むこと。

● 1 次試験免除

前回または前々回の 1 次試験に合格し，2 次試験に不合格または欠席した場合，申請により 1 次試験が免除され，2 次試験のみ受験できる。申込書の所定欄にその旨を記入し申し込むこと。検定料は同じ。

受験票

申込書と検定料金の受理後，受験地の会場・所在地が記載された受験票が 1 次試験日の 1 週間前までに送付される。届かない場合は，必ず試験日の 3 日前までに国連英検事務局（03-6228-6831〈代表〉）へ問い合わせること。顔写真 1 枚（4センチ×3 センチ）を試験日までに用意し受験票に貼り付けておくこと。試験当日は，受験票とともに身分証明書を持参すること。

受験申し込み方法

書店，郵送，インターネット（PC・スマートフォン）で申し込みができる。

詳細は国連英検ホームページ http://www.kokureneiken.jp/ で確認する。

申込受付期間

第 1 回　3 月初旬〜4 月下旬　※翌日消印有効

第 2 回　8 月上旬〜9 月下旬　※翌日消印有効

検定料のお支払い方法

電話で申し込む場合	国連英検事務局へ電話・FAX にて申し込みができる。申し込み受付後「コンビニ支払用紙」が郵送される。
郵送で申し込む場合	国連英検事務局に受験申込書を請求する。 ●支払方法：必ず受験者氏名で銀行または郵便局から振り込む。
インターネット (PC・スマートフォン) で申し込む場合	国連英検のホームページから申し込みができる。 (PC・スマートフォン) http://www.kokureneiken.jp/ ●支払方法：クレジットカード支払い，コンビニエンスストア支払い，銀行または郵便局から振り込む。

検定料の各種支払詳細

振込の場合	●銀行からの振込 銀行名：　三菱 UFJ 銀行　日本橋支店 口座名：　(公財) 日本国際連合協会　国連英検事務局 口座番号：普通口座 0010400 金額：　　該当級の受験料 ※振込手数料は受験者負担。 ※現金・為替は取り扱い不可。 ※いずれも事務局が申込書と検定料の受領を確認後，受付完了。 ※インターネット (PC・スマートフォン) で申し込んだ受験者は，ご依頼人の前に「受付番号」(メールにて通知される) を記入する。
	●郵便局からの払込 郵便局設置の払込書 (青票) にて以下の内容を記入の上，払い込む。 加入者名：(公財) 日本国際連合協会 口座番号：00130-7-24670 金額：　　該当級の受験料 ※振込手数料は受験者負担。 ※ご依頼人欄に受験者名，住所，電話番号を必ず記入する。インターネット (PC・スマートフォン) で申し込んだ受験者は，ご依頼人の前に「受付番号」(メールにて通知される) を記入する。 ※払込金受領書は必ず保管する。
クレジットカード の場合	●インターネット (PC・スマートフォン) からの申し込みのみ可能 入力フォームにて「クレジットカード払い」を選択し，カード番号，有効期限などを入力する。 ※利用可能クレジットカードは国連英検のホームページで確認のこと。
コンビニエンスストア の場合	●インターネット (PC・スマートフォン) からの申し込みの場合 入力フォームにて「コンビニ払い」を選択すると，払込票が送付される。 ●電話・FAX で申し込みの場合 申し込み受付完了後事務局より「コンビニ支払用紙」が郵送される。 ※全国の主要なコンビニエンスストアにて受験料を支払う。

著者・執筆協力者プロフィール

著　者

髙 橋 信 道（たかはし・のぶみち）
翻訳家。京都大学理学部および文学部卒。国連英検指導検討委員会委員。
著書に『国連英検過去問題集特 A 級・A 級』（共著，三修社）他。

長　和 重（ちょう・かずしげ）
高崎経済大学講師。敬和学園大学講師。国連英検指導検討委員会委員。著
書に『国連ニュースで読む世界』（共著，三修社），『国連英検過去問題集特
A 級・A 級』（共著，三修社）他。

石 渡 淳 元（いしわた・あつもと）
早稲田大学政治経済学部卒。国連英検指導検討委員会委員。訳書に
『WAL-MART エグい会社に知恵で勝つ！』（インデックス・コミュニケー
ションズ），著書に『国連ニュースで読む世界』（共著，三修社），『国連英
検過去問題集特 A 級・A 級』（共著，三修社）他。

Lawrence Karn（ローレンス・カーン）
大妻女子大学特任教授。成城大学講師。学術博士。国連英検指導検討委員
会委員長。論文に「Developing English Skills by Reporting on Current
Events and World News」（OJSIS），著書に『国連英検過去問題集特 A
級・A 級』（共著，三修社）他。

執筆協力者

服 部 孝 彦（はっとり・たかひこ）
大妻女子大学・同大学院教授。早稲田大学講師。言語学博士。国連英検統括監修官。著書に『国連英検ベーシック・トライアル』（三修社）など多数。

武 藤 克 彦（むとう・かつひこ）
東洋英和女学院大学准教授。国連英検指導検討委員会委員長。著書に『国連英検特 A 級・A 級対策［改訂版］』（共著，三修社),『上級時事英文法』（三修社）など多数。

Paul Underwood（ポール・アンダーウッド）
東洋英和女学院大学教授。言語学博士。国連英検指導検討委員会委員。著書に『EFL Reading in Japan: Theory, Policy, and Practice』（メディアイランド）他，英語教育関係の論文多数。

Gordon Myskow（ゴードン・ミスコウ）
神田外語大学大学院准教授。応用言語学博士。国連英検指導検討委員会委員。著書に『EFL Writing in Japan: Theory, Policy, and Practice』（メディアイランド）他，英語教育関係の論文多数。

こくれんえいけんかこもんだいしゅう　えーきゅう　　　　　　　　　　　　　　　　　　　　　　　　ねんどじっし
国連英検過去問題集 ［A級］〈2019-2020年度実施〉

2021年8月31日　第1刷発行

編　者	公益財団法人　日本国際連合協会
著　者	髙橋信道　長和重　石渡淳元　ローレンス・カーン
執筆協力	服部孝彦　武藤克彦　ポール・アンダーウッド　ゴードン・ミスコウ
発行者	前田俊秀
発行所	株式会社三修社
	〒150-0001　東京都渋谷区神宮前2-2-22
	TEL 03-3405-4511　FAX 03-3405-4522
	振替 00190-9-72758
	https://www.sanshusha.co.jp
	編集協力／編集工房キャパ
印刷・製本	日経印刷株式会社

©2021 United Nations Association of Japan　Printed in Japan
ISBN978-4-384-06002-7 C2082